24/7

LIVING FOR GOD IN REAL LIFE

TIM LEV...

simply for students

"From the moment you wake up until late night, and everything in between—the locker at school, the cafeteria, the library, after-school activities—Tim gives down-to-earth guidance that will help you bring more of heaven into your life and those around you. Caution: This book will guide you to a life worth living."

— JR Woodward, National Director, V3 Church Planting Movement; Author, *Creating a Missional Culture*

"Tim has always been just a really good writer. When he told me he was writing this book I just knew it would be best thing ever written on this topic. He's such a sweet boy."

— Peggy (Tim's mom)

"Parents of teenagers regularly ask me for help choosing a devotional or book that their teenager can read to be encouraged spiritually. I'm exciting to finally have a book I can recommend that I really believe in. Youth ministers should buy this book by the case for their students. Great job, Tim!"

— Jeremy Lee, Creator of ParentMinistry.net

"I'm not surprised Timmy wrote a book. It probably has graphs and charts and diagrams in it. You know, I used to call him Cabbage Head; I guess he needed an oversized head to hold in his big, nerdy brain. Way to go, Cab!"

— Shane (Tim's older brother)

DEDICATION //

This book is dedicated to my princesses, Elle, Zoe, and Ashton. May you always pursue the life of wonder and amazement that is only found in the kingdom of God.

ACKNOWLEDGMENTS //

First and always, I'm thankful to the God who loved me before anyone else and believes in me more than I believe in myself. I pray God continues to renovate my imagination as I cooperate with his Spirit to live and reveal his kingdom in my own life.

I can never thank my sweet wife enough. She puts up with all of the things I hide from everyone else and seems to love me and my eccentricities anyway. I love you, babe, and I love our life.

Many thanks to friends and colleagues with whom I've been blessed to have countless conversations over the last 20 years. This book is the product of many of them.

"I want a lifetime of holy moments. Every day I want to be in dangerous proximity to Jesus. I long for a life that explodes with meaning and is filled with adventure, wonder, risk, and danger. I long for a faith that is gloriously treacherous."

– Mike Yaconelli, *Dangerous Wonder*

24/7
Living for God in Real Life

© 2015 Tim Levert

group.com
simplyyouthministry.com

All rights reserved. No part of this book may be reproduced in any manner whatsoever without prior written permission from the publisher, except where noted in the text and in the case of brief quotations embodied in critical articles and reviews. For information, visit group.com/customer-support/permissions.

CREDITS
Author: Tim Levert
Executive Developer: Tim Gilmour
Chief Creative Officer: Joani Schultz
Editor: Rob Cunningham
Cover Art and Production: Veronica Preston
Illustrator: Tasha Levert
Project Manager: Stephanie Krajec

Unless otherwise indicated, Scripture quotations are taken from the Holy Bible, New Living Translation, copyright ©1996, 2004, 2007, 2013 by Tyndale House Foundation. Used by permission of Tyndale House Publishers, Inc., Carol Stream, Illinois 60188. All rights reserved.

Scripture quotations marked THE MESSAGE from *THE MESSAGE*. Copyright © by Eugene H. Peterson 1993, 1994, 1995, 1996, 2000, 2001, 2002. Used by permission of NavPress Publishing Group.

Scripture marked NLV taken from the Holy Bible, New Life Version, Copyright © 1969-2003 by Christian Literature International, P.O. Box 777, Canby, Oregon, 97013. Used by permission.

Scripture quotations marked HCSB are taken from the Holman Christian Standard Bible®, Copyright © 1999, 2000, 2002, 2003, 2009 by Holman Bible Publishers. Used by permission. HCSB® is a federally registered trademark of Holman Bible Publishers.

ISBN: 978-0-7644-8286-1

10 9 8 7 6 5 4 3 2 1   21 20 19 18 17 16 15

Printed in the U.S.A.

TABLE OF CONTENTS

INTRODUCTION.. 1

A NOTE TO PARENTS, YOUTH LEADERS
AND OTHER ADULTS.. 6

CHAPTER 1 //
BEDHEAD, TOOTHPASTE, AND ALARM CLOCKS........ 8

CHAPTER 2 //
POP-TARTS, CHEERIOS, AND SPILLED MILK 21

CHAPTER 3 //
TARDY BELLS AND HOMEROOM 31

CHAPTER 4 //
COMBINATION LOCKS AND CANDY WRAPPERS 39

CHAPTER 5 //
MYSTERY MEAT AND MILK-IN-A-BOX 48

CHAPTER 6 //
DUSTY BOOKS AND "QUIET PLEASE" 61

CHAPTER 7 //
TEAM CHEERS, OVERTIME, AND ARPEGGIOS 74

CHAPTER 8 //
STAYING UP LATE AND SLEEPING IN 85

CHAPTER 9 //
SERMON NOTES AND SUNDAY SCHOOL................ 95

CHAPTER 10 //
FLIRTING, COURTING, AND GOING STEADY 104

CHAPTER 11 //
WHAT DO YOU WANT TO BE WHEN
YOU GROW UP?..121

FINAL THOUGHTS 136

24/7

What if you lived and revealed the Kingdom of God 24/7

Act justly. Love mercy. Walk humbly with God.

Love everybody. Serve people.

B Forgive. Play well with others. Be encouraging.

Be thankful. Wait your turn.

Smile at grumpy people. Lark.

Accept people who look, smell and think differently than you. Don't bite. Listen. Trust.

Chase after Jesus. Share ur gum. Shine. Dance.

Live life to the full. Defend the weak. Sing. Laugh. Dream.

Be salt. Be light. Speak out.

Give more and take less. Love. Be the real you!

Be the change your friends need. Live in freedom. Lark.

Say yes to the call. Live fearlessly.

Live truth. Believe there is more to this life than what you see.

By: Tim Levert

INTRODUCTION //

Hi. I'm not sure why you picked up this book, but I'm really glad you did. **I believe this is the most important book you'll ever read.**

OK, that's probably a stretch. **But it could be the most important book you read this week!**

If you're open to dreaming a little, I believe God can use this book to help you see what your life *could* be like if you lived the way God wanted 24 hours a day, 7 days a week. But it will take some imagination.

This book is about living and revealing the kingdom of God (we'll shorten this phrase to **LaRK** throughout the book) every moment of every day. The kingdom of God is a big deal. It's life the way God dreamed for us to live, filled with wonder, purpose, passion, joy, and his presence. Jesus is the perfect example of living and revealing God's kingdom—he did everything exactly the way God wanted. And as Jesus' followers, we are invited to trust Jesus enough to live the way he lived—the way of God's kingdom.

TBH But very little of this stuff is easy. And I don't want to give you "fluffy" answers that dodge the "real life" stuff that you may be thinking. **Anytime you see this little picture (TBH), I'm trying to cut through the fake and get down to what you really, honestly might be thinking.**

A lot of this stuff comes down to trust. Do you *trust* that God's way is best? It's not about obeying rules and staying out of trouble; it's about imagining what life could be like if we lived it God's way.

Because everything we do as followers of Jesus ought to be about living and revealing God's kingdom.

This book is all about helping you live and reveal God's kingdom in the "everyday" moments of life.

Many people in today's culture assume the worst about teenagers. You are expected to have lots of sex, do a lot of partying, and generally be really selfish. You are expected to fail, because you don't have the strength to do the right thing.

And I completely reject those ideas.

I believe that when God gets ahold of your heart and your imagination, amazing things happen. I believe you can learn to see the world as God see it, and live life the same way Jesus lived. When Jesus told his disciples that they would do even greater things than he did (John 14), he was looking at a group mostly made up of teenagers.

I don't believe you are the church of tomorrow; I believe you are the church of today. And the church needs you.

My prayer is that you will read this book with an open heart and an inspired imagination.

==What would your life look like if you lived it the way Jesus did—the way God wants you to live—24/7?==

I'd love to hear from you. About this book, about your life, about your own journey. Shoot me an email at 247book@gmail.com, and let's keep the conversation going.

WHAT IF?

Jesus, please clear my mind of the old ways I used to live, and renovate my imagination to see what life could be if I trusted you in all things. May your Spirit give me courage to say no to "I can't," and open my eyes to catch a vision of "what if?" Inspire me by your life, death, and resurrection to live a life that reveals God's kingdom 24/7. In your name, amen.

Meet Dennis. Dennis is a normal guy. He's smart and good-looking, a decent athlete, funny, and sorta popular. He really wishes he was more popular, though, and he tries everything he can think of to climb the ranks of the popular students at his school. On most weekends, Dennis attends a local church with his family, but he's not really into it, because he's not sure how Jesus would affect his popularity. Dennis knows a lot about the Bible, but he's not sure what he really believes—he's too worried about what his friends at school will think about him. Dennis is a good guy, but he's missing out on the life God dreams for him. And deep down, he knows it.

Meet Dustin. Dustin is a normal guy, too. In fact, he's a lot like Dennis. He's smart, good-looking, not a great athlete (but a legit musician), funny (funnier than Dennis), and almost as popular as Dennis. And like Dennis, Dustin wishes he were more popular, too. But recently something changed. A few months ago, Dustin went to visit his family in another state. While there, he went to his cousin's youth group, and Dustin committed his life to Jesus. Dustin doesn't know a lot about the Bible, but he's growing. And he keeps asking God to help him see things differently. And strangely enough, God seems to be answering him.

Last thing. **Try to read this book with a pencil handy.** There are lots of places for you to interact with things, and I believe the more you're willing to play along, the more you'll get out of this book. Even if you think some of this stuff is cheesy, give it a shot anyway! You might be surprised at what God does in your life when you live and reveal his kingdom.

THIS BOOK BELONGS TO:

WRITE YOUR NAME:
_____

WRITE THE NAME YOU WISH YOUR PARENTS WOULD HAVE GIVEN YOU:
_____

GIVE YOURSELF A SUPERHERO POWER AND NAME HERE:
_____

WRITE YOUR NAME IN YOUR FAVORITE FONT:
_____

SING ON THE X:
X_____

A NOTE //

TO PARENTS, YOUTH LEADERS, AND OTHER ADULTS WHO CARE ABOUT TEENAGERS:

Being the parent of an adolescent is a constant challenge, and helping them grow in their trust in God can feel impossible.

This book is all about living and revealing the kingdom of God. The kingdom of God is a big deal. It represents God's plan for his creation—living life the way God dreamed for us, filled with wonder, purpose, passion, joy, and God!

As followers of Jesus, we are invited to trust him enough to live the way he lived—the way of God's kingdom. We love, we serve, we give, we forgive, we laugh, we grieve, we live well. Sometimes it's really difficult, but it's always worth it. Because as we live the kingdom of God, others will see it, and maybe they will want find their place in God's kingdom, too.

Everything we do as followers of Jesus can be about living and revealing God's kingdom. This book is all about helping teenagers live and reveal God's kingdom in the "everyday" moments of life, 24/7.

You may read that and think, "That *sounds* great, Tim, but it's awfully idealistic to expect that *everything* teenagers do will be about God's kingdom."

I agree—it is totally idealistic. But I believe young people often meet the expectations placed on them.

Culture expects students to fail: reckless sexuality, substance use/abuse, selfishness, and so on. I believe we can encourage and expect teenagers to live and reveal God's kingdom.

It's OK to push teenagers to be missional—they can do it.

Being missional is the understanding that God created the church—his called-out people—to continue his mission to redeem and restore all things. Living missionally means we engage the world the same way God does—by carrying the mission of God into every sphere of life.

Parents, one more thing: I believe the best way you can help your teenager grow as a follower of Jesus is to follow Jesus yourself. If you're hoping they'll "do as you say, not as you do," you're setting them up to struggle. Please allow me to encourage you to invest (or reinvest) yourself in your own relationship with Jesus and make a renewed commitment to live and reveal God's kingdom.

I'd love to hear from you. About this book, about your teenager, about your own journey. Shoot me an email at 247book@gmail.com, and let's keep the conversation going.

CHAPTER 1 //

BEDHEAD, TOOTHPASTE, AND ALARM CLOCKS

The buzzing in your ears grows louder and louder and louder. You try to ignore it, but it's not stopping.

Then you realize it's your alarm clock.

Is it really morning already? Didn't you just fall asleep? Why do morning people get to decide when school starts, anyway? Ugh.

You may not have a written list of "things to do to get ready" before school, but you probably do the same things every day. They're habits you've done so often that they're almost automatic in your life—you do them without even thinking.

If you haven't already, I'd encourage you to add a few spiritual "things to do" to your list, too—things that you do every day to get ready to see God's kingdom around you and be ready to respond. (If that sentence is confusing, take a minute and read the introduction.)

THINGS TO DO TO GET READY:

1.
2.
3.
4.
5.
6.
7.
8.
9.
10.

When we develop habits that help us practice hearing from God in private, it makes it a lot easier to see God's kingdom in public and know how to respond.

For the rest of this chapter, I want to share some things you can do to help you deepen your trust in God. None of these things are magic, but if you open yourself to God's presence in your life, cool stuff will happen.

SPEND UNINTERRUPTED TIME WITH JESUS

Lots of us have a person or two in our lives that we text or call as soon as we wake up. Maybe it's your parent, your BFF, your sweetie, or your younger sibling that you "accidentally" wake up every morning as you're getting dressed.

What would it look like if you added Jesus to that list? Would it surprise you to know that he wants to be on that list? Did you know that Jesus loves us so much that he never stops thinking about us—even when we're sleeping!?

"*How precious are your thoughts about me, O God. They cannot be numbered! I can't even count them; they outnumber the grains of sand! And when I wake up, you are still with me!*" (Psalm 139:17-18).

GOD wants to spend time with you.

God **WANTS** to spend time with you.

God wants to spend **TIME** with you.

God wants to spend time with **YOU**.

God wants to hear every word you say, every time you want to say it.

You never talk too much for God. God never gets tired of hearing from you.

In Matthew 7:7, Jesus told his followers, *"Keep on asking, and you will receive what you ask for. Keep on seeking, and you will find. Keep on knocking, and the door will be opened to you."*

TBH *I struggle with this whole idea. How do you spend time with Jesus when you can't see him or hear him?*

This is one of the best questions about Jesus. And I don't have a great answer, because we can't see him. But he is always with us.

"And be sure of this: I [Jesus] am with you always, even to the end of the age" (Matthew 28:20).

Part of our relationship with Jesus is trusting that he is with us, even when it doesn't feel like it.

TALK WITH JESUS

When we decide to spend time with Jesus, what do we talk about?

About his goodness. God has done some pretty amazing things for us. Take some time to thank Jesus for them—not because God is insecure and needs us to give him props but because it reminds us of the good things he's done. Write down one of your favorite "God stories" on the next page.

About your life. Jesus loves you and cares about the things that are important to you. So talk with him about anything and everything that is important to you.

Tell Jesus about all the things that you're excited about, the things that you're worried about, the things that you need help with, the things that are going great. Talk to Jesus like you're talking to a friend—because you are.

About other people. Jesus cares for us and wants us to care for others. It's not always easy, because sometimes the stuff in our lives seems so big we don't have time to worry about others.

Try anyway!

You might be surprised at what Jesus does in your life when you spend time talking with him about others.

Spend some time each day talking with him about your family. Ask him to help your parents be the kind of parents he wants them to be. Ask him to help your siblings make good decisions. And ask Jesus to help you live and reveal God's kingdom in your family.

Spend some time each day talking with Jesus about your friends. You probably have a friend or two going through a difficult time—ask Jesus to help them out. You may have another friend who doesn't know Jesus yet—ask him to give you an opportunity to have a spiritual conversation. You might have another friend who just found out some super amazing news—thank Jesus on their behalf.

Spend time each day talking with Jesus about leaders in your life: parents, teachers, school administrators, coaches, government leaders, and so on. Around the picture below, write the names of adults and students at your school that God is nudging you to pray for.

About things that matter to you. Spend some time talking with Jesus about anything that matters to you. Maybe it's a cause like human trafficking or childhood cancer; maybe you've been on a mission trip to a place like Haiti, and your heart is broken for all the orphans there. Whatever issue maters to you, talk with Jesus about it.

LISTEN TO JESUS

A conversation isn't just one-way: Sometimes we talk, and sometimes we listen. A conversation with Jesus works the same way.

It's important that we spend lots of time talking to Jesus. But how do we listen for his response?

The Bible. I believe the Bible is the most important book in your life. It also can be the most misunderstood: It's huge, it was originally written in languages you don't speak, it talks about people who lived long ago, and it contains some weird stories!

First, start with a translation you can understand. Most pastors and youth leaders will be happy that you're reading the Bible, and they'll be glad to help you find a version that makes sense to you.

Second, have a plan. You can find lots of different reading plans online, or ask someone you trust about their Bible-reading plan.

Third, stick to it. Some parts of the Bible are easy to read, but some are strange. You will probably find some things that confuse you and bring up questions—that's awesome! Write down where you're stumped, and go talk to someone about it!

TBH

I'm not sure where to start reading in the Bible. I tried to start at the beginning, but by the time I got to Leviticus, I was lost! Where should I start?

Any order is a good order, as long as you're reading the Bible. I recommend that you start reading in this order:

// Gospel of John
// Proverbs
// James
// Genesis
// Romans
// Psalms

Once you're done with these, go talk to your pastor or youth leader about where to go from there!

A daily devotional. A super easy way to get started listening to Jesus is by using a daily devotional—a one-page(ish)-per day reading that usually has some combination of a daily Bible verse, a paragraph or so explanation, something to do in response, a prayer, and a challenging wrap-up.

A book like this. Books written for teenagers to help you grow deeper in their faith can be hard to come by, so give a hearty thanks to whoever gave this one to you. Keep reading this one—then find another one, then another one.

Your heart. Our hearts can be easily misled, so my huge caveat for this idea is that anything God nudges you to do in your heart will be in agreement with what God says in the Bible. In other words, God will never lead you to do something that goes against the Bible.

Just because you feel something in your heart doesn't necessarily mean it's from God or that you should do it.

But I do believe God impresses things on our hearts to help us understand what he wants for our lives.

WRITE THINGS DOWN

Over the course of my life as a Christ-follower, God has taught me a ton of lessons, but I don't remember the specifics of all of them. And I wish I did. If I'd written them down, I'd have a record of God's faithfulness over the past 25 years.

RECENT LESSONS I'VE LEARNED:

Lessons learned. When God teaches you a lesson—the easy way or the hard way—write it down, including the details of the story: How old were you? What was going on in your life? Why did God teach you the lesson? What was the lesson? Without all those details, you may lose some sweet memories of God's goodness.

Prayer list. I know there have been times I've told people I would pray for them, but when I got home, I forgot what I was supposed to be praying for. Keeping a prayer list is an old-fashioned-but-really-effective way of remembering who and what I'm praying for.

Answered prayer list. Prayer is about way more than God saying yes or no, but I do believe God answers our specific prayers. When he does, write it down. Sometimes you'll write down, "God said no," but sometimes you'll get to write, "God said yes!"

DUSTIN AND DENNIS

Dennis (read the introduction) occasionally starts the morning by reading a daily devotion, but it never goes deeper than a passing thought. He reads it, mentally checks it off his to-do list, feels a little better about himself, and goes on about his day, not really thinking about Jesus until the next morning. He means well, but he's never really reoriented his life around a relationship with Jesus.

Dustin (again, read the introduction) starts a few days each week by reading a daily devotion, but he rarely stops thinking about Jesus, talking to Jesus throughout the day, and looking for ways to live out God's kingdom. He knows he could do better, but he really tries to love and trust Jesus a little more every day.

TBH

I'm doing some of these things already, and I don't feel like I've grown very much. In fact, I feel like I'm stuck. What am I missing?

I wish there was a formula for trusting Jesus more, but there isn't. In fact, practicing the spiritual habits listed in this chapter won't guarantee that you'll see or hear Jesus or grow deeper in your trust. But if you put your heart into it and ask him to help you, your relationship with Jesus will grow. And I believe when you get closer to Jesus, you will learn that you can trust him more.

ONE MORE THING

Before you walk out of your room for the day, take a minute and pray a prayer like this:

God, today is your day. You made it, you're giving it to me as a gift, and you have things for me to do today. Help me follow your leading, live your kingdom out today in the things I say and do, and reveal your kingdom to the people in my life. In Jesus' name, amen.

Now go have some breakfast.

CHAPTER 2 //

POP-TARTS, CHEERIOS, AND SPILLED MILK

You shuffle down the hall to the kitchen to eat breakfast. You don't really like breakfast, and you're pretty sure that whole "breakfast is the most important meal of the day" thing is just a clever ploy by your parents[1] to get you to eat cereal that tastes like cardboard. But you do it anyway.

You're late, so the rest of your family is already eating. It's all you can do not to plead your case again on the importance of sleep and the need to go back to bed for more rest. Instead, you grunt something that resembles a "g'mrnin'," pour yourself some cereal, and sit down.

1: I use the word *parents* throughout this chapter, but depending on your family situation, it might mean "parent" or "grandparent" or "aunt" or "uncle" or any other adult who cares for you.

MY TYPICAL BREAKFAST

TBH

My family never eats breakfast together. My parents and siblings all go off in different directions while hardly acknowledging one another. I can skip this chapter, right?

Most of us don't have a "sit down" breakfast time with our families—if you do, thank your parents. But you do have some interaction with them each day. As you read through this chapter, don't dismiss what I'm saying if an example doesn't fit perfectly. Use your creative muscles and connect the dots between what I'm saying and what your life looks like.

A SOLID FOUNDATION

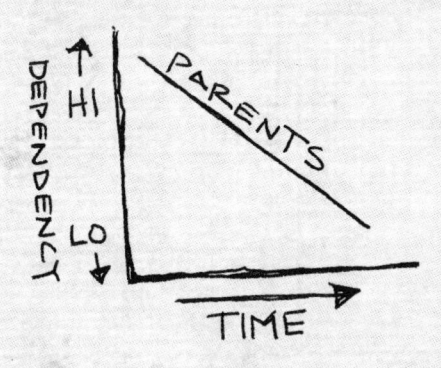

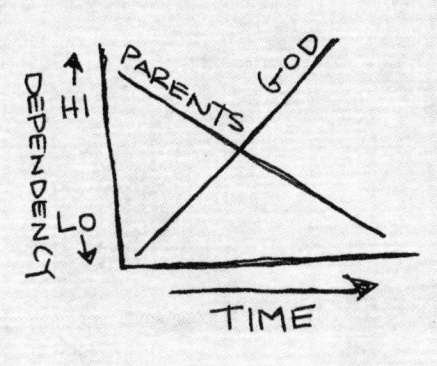

Many people mistakenly view growing up as you (the child) becoming less dependent on your parents.

That IS part of the story, but it's not the whole story. As a follower of Jesus, growing up means becoming less dependent on your parents *as you* become more dependent on God.

Sometimes your parents hit it out of the park, and they do a great job helping you with this transition. But sometimes your parents strike out. (Maybe cut them some slack.)

The truth is, even if they struggle to admit it, your parents know they're not perfect. But most parents are doing the best they can. Allow this Scripture to challenge you to start thinking and living differently:

"Honor your father and mother. Then you will live a long, full life in the land the Lord your God is giving you" (Exodus 20:12).

> **STUFF MY PARENTS TAUGHT ME:**

What if you decided to stop thinking about the things you didn't like and focused instead on reasons you can be thankful for your family? Here are a few things to get your creative muscles going.

SAY AND WRITE NICE THINGS

Take a minute and list on the next page all the things that your parents do for you: provide a place to live and all the little things that go with that (shampoo, toothpaste, toilet paper), buy and cook food to eat, buy and clean clothes, provide transportation, give allowance or spending money, buy gifts, take you on trips, and so on. Bonus points for having more than 20 things on your list!

Space to Brainstorm

What if you started saying "thank you" every time your parents did something for you?

Even for the really small things that seem unimportant. And once a week (or so), what if you wrote them a note telling them how thankful you are for something—anything—they've done for you that week?

BE RESPONSIBLE

Teenagers who grow up having household chores are much less likely to be jerks than students who don't have anything to do.

(That is my interpretation of a lot of scientific reports. And it's spot on.)

If you don't have household chores, ask for some. Or take the initiative to look around your house, and when you see something that needs to be done, just do it.

If you do have chores, what if you did them without being asked? And what if you took some initiative and started doing other things around the house that needed to be done?

WATCH YOUR ATTITUDE

We all struggle with our attitude at some point. It's natural and human to not be happy when someone asks you to do something that you don't want to do. Or if they ask you not to do something you want.

It's totally OK to start out having a bad attitude in your mind. But it's totally *not* OK to stay there.

"Do everything without complaining and arguing" (Philippians 2:14).

But how do we DO that?

"You must have the same attitude that Christ Jesus had" (Philippians 2:5).

Jesus deserved to be treated as royalty, to be spoiled, and to be worshipped. But he chose to serve with an attitude of humility. If this is connecting with you, grab a Bible or Bible app and read all of Philippians 2—it's pretty challenging.

What if you started doing the things your parents asked without complaining?

What if the next time they told you no, you said, "no problem"? What if you made having a positive attitude your personal goal with your parents?

DUSTIN AND DENNIS

Dennis thinks he should get to do whatever he wants whenever he wants because he's almost an adult. He doesn't think his parents should ever say no or should ask him to do things he doesn't want to do. If Dennis doesn't want to do something, he'll complain the whole time he's doing it—and probably for a few days after he's done.

Like Dennis, Dustin wants to do what he wants to do. He's a normal teenager, and when his parents ask him to do something, he thinks, "Stank! I really don't want to do that!" But before he opens his mouth, he remembers something he read in a daily devotion, where God said we should honor our parents. So Dustin simply says, "no problem," and does what his parents ask with the best attitude he can manage.

PRAY

If you're like me, it's easy to pray when things are falling apart. And it's easy to pray about stuff that's important to you. But if you're like me, you might not always think about praying for others, even the people you share a house with. In the house on the next page, write the names of everyone who lives with you.

What if you committed to start each day by praying for everyone on that list? What if you asked God to bless them in whatever they're doing, to help them manage all the pressures of life, and to help you honor them in everything you say and do? What do you think God might do in *your* life if you began praying for your family (including your parents) every day?

BE AN EXAMPLE

Everyone in your family is on a spiritual journey, just as you are. I have heard quite a few stories of teenagers who were the only Christ-follower in their families but eventually helped their parents or siblings place their trust in Jesus.

What kind of influence are you having on your family?

Whether you have older or younger siblings, because you share a home with them, you have an opportunity to be an example and influence them like no one else in their lives.

"Don't let anyone think less of you because you are young. Be an example to all believers in what you say, in the way you live, in your love, your faith, and your purity" (1 Timothy 4:12).

What if you began doing all the things in this chapter, and your siblings started following your lead? How might your family be different if you committed to living and revealing God's kingdom with your own family?

TBH *My family isn't great. To be honest, I think I hate my family. What am I supposed to do with that?*

This whole "love your family" bit might be the hardest chapter to live out. Maybe it's because your family knows you at your best and your worst. But I believe making sense of your family relationships is a key part of living and revealing God's kingdom outside of your home 24/7.

The good news: God will help you if you ask, and you can do it!

ONE MORE THING

If you're struggling to get motivated about this chapter, ask yourself, "What needs in my family might God want me to meet?" and "What would my family look like if God's kingdom was lived out?" The way you think about the whole process might be helpful as you try to live out God's kingdom in your family.

Now, go brush your teeth; they're furry!

CHAPTER 3 //

TARDY BELLS AND HOMEROOM

I hate school. My wife hates it, too. We despise it. And my kids hate school. And I'm pretty sure even my dog hates school.

Just to be clear, I love learning, but I hate school. I love reading, I love doing nerdy math equations, and I really liked most of my teachers, especially Mrs. D—she is my all-time favorite—but I hate school.

DISCLAIMER: I know school is important. Stay in school, work hard, and earn your diploma. School should be one of your top priorities.

But I still hate it.

But I love people. The best part of school was getting to see my friends. I would even show up a little early just so I could hang out with them. But I didn't like *everyone* at my school. And I didn't want to hang out with everyone. Just my friends.

And sometimes, my friends and I could be less than kind to certain teachers or students. In fact, we could be downright mean. Even after I started following Jesus in the 10th grade, I still had some ugliness inside of me that fell out on occasion.

But why does any of that matter? Most of the people at school, you only see at school. You're not really friends with them, you're not going to hang out with them, and they probably have plenty of friends already.

And teachers and administrators—who cares? They're all adults, and they don't have any problems or insecurities. They don't care about what you think about them or say to them, do they?

Ms. Effingham

Or do they? What if your words *do* matter to them? And what responsibility is it of yours to worry about that, anyway?

What does it mean to live and reveal God's kingdom at school? As a follower of Jesus, what things could you be thinking about as you spend your day at school?

EVERYONE DESERVES RESPECT

God makes it pretty clear in the Bible that we are made in his image:

"So God created human beings in his own image. In the image of God he created them; male and female he created them" (Genesis 1:27).

That verse means that while we are not God and will never be God, we have the capacity to display God-like qualities—we can show love, compassion, creativity, joy, passion, purpose, and peace.

It means that as humans, we hold a unique place among all of creation, because we are made in the image of God.

WOW

It means that there's nothing we can do that will make us any more valuable to God than we already are, because we are his.

And as followers of Jesus, it means we need to recognize this built-in worth of all people and show them respect, simply because we are all made in God's image.

TBH

Not everyone at my school seems to get this idea. Some people do things and say things that aren't very Christ-like. In fact, some people reject the very idea that there is a God. How should I treat people like this?

First, I would guess that you sometimes do things and say things that aren't very Christ-like, too. I sure have. And we want people to show us respect, right?

Second, if a platypus decided that it wasn't a platypus anymore but was an eagle, how well would it do if it jumped off a cliff? I'm pretty sure it would become a splatypus. (See what I did there?) Just because a platypus denies its identity doesn't change the nature of what it is. And just because someone denies their identity as God's creation or even denies God's existence, that doesn't change what's true. Truth must determine how we live as kingdom people. And the truth is, everyone deserves respect—even people we don't like.

We don't respect people because they deserve it; we respect people because God created them. And God is inviting us to partner with him by living lives that reveal his kingdom.

"And to all these things, you must add love. Love holds everything and everybody together and makes all these good things perfect" (Colossians 3:14, NLV).

YOUR SCHOOL IS YOUR PARISH

John Wesley was a pretty big deal in church life back in the day, and he wrote some pretty amazing things. One of his most famous quotes was, "I look upon all the world as my parish." In this quote, "parish" meant the area a pastor was responsible for caring for. Wesley was saying that as a follower of Jesus, he viewed every person he encountered as someone he should care about and care for.

JOHN WESLEY   BALD JOHN WESLEY

I think that's pretty amazing.

And I believe *your* school is *your* parish.

I believe every person you encounter from your school is someone Jesus wants you to care about and care for. In a way, you're a "campus pastor"—and maybe, just maybe, God has placed you in your school for a specific purpose.

YOU ARE THE ONLY HOPE IN SOME PEOPLE'S LIVES

We live in a messed-up world. Relationships are broken, people are cruel, and teenagers and adults experience pain that they should never experience.

And for some people, no one in their lives treats them with respect and shows them love.

But Jesus has given you the opportunity to spend several hours each day with people who are hoping to find someone who lives life differently:

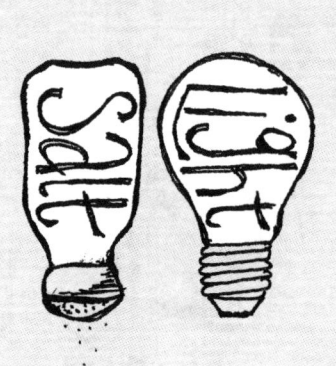

"Let me tell you why you are here. You're here to be salt-seasoning that brings out the God-flavors of this earth. ... Here's another way to put it: You're here to be light, bringing out the God-colors in the world" (Matthew 5:13-14, THE MESSAGE).

Jesus isn't suggesting that you create something that isn't there. You're not *bringing* God somewhere he's not already at work. You're highlighting what God's *already doing* on your campus and in people's lives.

TBH

This feels pretty weird to me. I'm not sure I know how to bring out God-flavors or God-colors. I'm not even sure what that means.

First, check out Chapter 1 of this book. I am convinced that the best way to see God and his kingdom (God-flavors and God-colors) in *public* is to practice seeing it in *private*. Chapter 1 helps you understand what this looks like.

Second, if you live like Jesus did and love people like Jesus does, you are bringing out God-flavors and God-colors. It's not complicated, but it does require commitment and trust.

DUSTIN AND DENNIS

Right now, Dennis is thinking, "Who cares if I tease people at school now and then? I can't help it if my sense of humor hurts people feelings—they should toughen up! And teachers are mean to me—they don't care what I think. Besides, words don't really mean anything."

But Dustin realizes that words matter, and even if everyone else at school talks trash about other people, he's going to do his best to avoid it. Dustin also knows that people might start teasing him if he doesn't play along and disrespect adults and tease other students. But Dustin has decided that he wants to partner with Jesus to see his school change.

ONE MORE THING

If you're not sure how to respond to this chapter, start praying for the people at your school. You don't have to *feel* like praying for people to actually pray for them. God can change the way you feel about people as you pray for them.

PRAY

If you're really bold, ask people how you can pray for them. Maybe say something like, "Jesus has been working on my heart about being more loving, and I've started praying for people at school. Is there something I could pray for you about?"

Who knows what Jesus is already doing in people's lives? His nudge for you to pray for people could be just what they need to hear so they can take a step forward in their own relationship with him. And you would get a taste of what it means to live a life that reveals God's kingdom 24/7.

Now, go to school.

CHAPTER 4 //

COMBINATION LOCKS AND CANDY WRAPPERS

I have a confession: I am combination lock-impaired.

My lack of combination lock skills made going to my locker in school pretty stressful, because I never knew if I would be able to get my math book.

I'm a believer in the lock-mess monster.

In my high school, we had seven minutes between classes, so I went to my locker several times each day. And because my campus was pretty small, even if I had to slay the lock-mess monster, I often had time for a three- or four-minute conversation before heading to class.

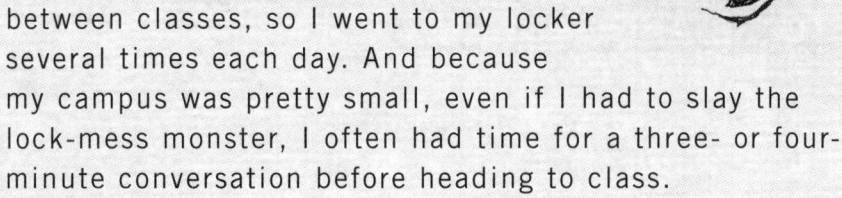

A few minutes a few times a day may not sound like enough time to have a conversation about things that matters. Maybe, but I believe if you view your locker conversations as an opportunity to help people see

God's kingdom just a little bit more clearly, a brief conversation might be just enough of an introduction for your friends to want to have a longer conversation later.

EACH DAY IS PART OF A LARGER CONVERSATION

In high school, my foreign language teacher had a French proverb on her classroom wall that said, "Petit à petit, l'oiseau fait son nid"—"little by little, the bird builds his nest." I know it's weird, and I never learned French, but the proverb makes sense. It means big things take time.

Each daily conversation with a friend might not be earth-shaking in terms of what you talk about or how it impacts you, but a three- to four-minute conversation is part of something bigger that is happening in your friendship.

NOT EVERY CONVERSATION HAS TO BE ABOUT JESUS

One of the most important things you can do to honor God is to show your friends a well-lived life.

Share stories about the cool things you did last weekend, the fun you had hanging out with your family, and the ways you helped that elderly couple in your neighborhood.

Not every conversation has to be about Jesus, but every conversation can reflect your relationship with Jesus and your lifestyle as his follower. For some (maybe most) of your friends, you have to *show* them the kingdom of God before you can *tell* them about it. Normal, healthy conversations are a huge part of living and revealing God's kingdom to your friends.

TBH

If I'm a follower of Jesus, shouldn't I use every conversation as a way to bring people closer to Jesus?

Yes! But I don't think talking about Jesus is the only way you bring people closer to him. When you live the way Jesus lived and love the way Jesus loved, you *are* talking about Jesus, but you're using your whole life instead of just your words.

When God's Spirit nudges you, speak up! But God knows that some people need to see your life before they can listen to your words.

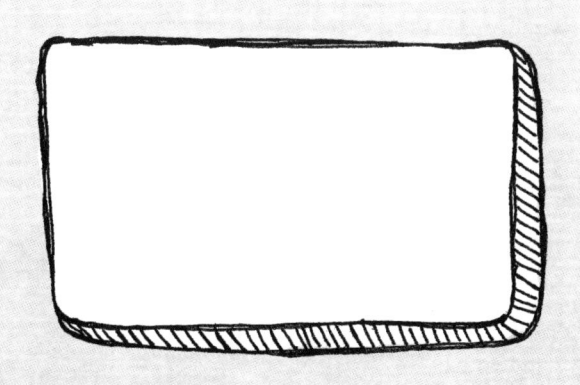

ASK ABOUT THEM

If you're talking to an athlete, ask about the big game. If your friend is in the band, ask about the upcoming competition. If she's a science lover, ask her to help you get to the bottom of string theory. If he's a fan of math, ask him to help you develop an algorithm to figure out what car you should buy.

As you get to know people, these conversations can get a little more personal. If you're talking to someone who's struggling at home, ask how things are going. If she has a family member who's been sick, ask how that person's doing. If he's celebrating something good in his life, be the first person to give him a high-five.

MY FRIEND'S NAME	MY FRIEND'S INTEREST

"I kept my bearings in Christ—but I entered their world and tried to experience things from their point of view. I've become just about every sort of servant there is in my attempts to lead those I meet into a God-saved life" (1 Corinthians 9:21-22, THE MESSAGE).

You're not being fake or manipulative; you're being a good friend who cares about what's important to the people in your life.

It's likely that some of your friends don't have anyone who's asking how *they're* doing.

You can give them a great gift by showing you care about what's important to them.

LOOK FOR GOD-MOMENTS

The coolest thing about conversations with your friends is that God is working in their lives: drawing them to follow Jesus, or helping them navigate a particularly difficult season of life, or challenging them to join you in living and revealing his kingdom at school.

But how do you know what God wants you to say or do?

"Never stop praying" (1 Thessalonians 5:17).

You can pray while you're in the middle of a conversation. In that situation, it's probably better if you pray in your mind instead of out loud, and it might be as simple as, "God, help me know what to say or do right now." God will help you know what to say or do—and when to say it or do it.

SHAPE THE CULTURE OF YOUR SCHOOL

Your school has a culture, and whether you like it or not, somehow, you are a part of it.

But just because you are a part of a culture doesn't mean you have to accept it as it is.

What will help change the culture of your school?

The way you treat people. Do you treat athletes better than you treat musicians? Do you treat hipsters better than you treat really smart students? Do you give most of your attention to the people your school culture has deemed popular?

This works in the other direction, too. Do you mistreat people whom your school culture has said are popular? In an effort to "balance the scale," do you treat unpopular people better than you treat popular people?

I'm not sure this approach is the best way to shape your school's culture either. Make the most of your time by treating all people well.

The way you respond to people. Not everyone at your school will like you. Shocking, I know. It's terrible.

It doesn't matter if you do the right things or the wrong things, if you hang out with the musicians or the really smart people, if you have a smartphone or a dumb phone. Someone will not like you for some reason.

"Don't let evil get the best of you; get the best of evil by doing good" (Romans 12:21, THE MESSAGE).

When people mistreat you—no matter the reason—continue to treat them well.

Show love and grace and patience and forgiveness. Just like Jesus treats us. Even in three-minute moments at your locker between classes.

DUSTIN AND DENNIS

Dennis views his locker conversations as times to build his reputation. He likes to crack jokes about people, he doesn't mind racist jokes, and he makes crude comments about girls as they walk by. He won't admit it, but he doesn't feel like his day is going well unless he makes people laugh. Dennis sometimes feels a little bad about his teasing, but he believes it's a part of who he is.

Dustin, on the other hand, has a great sense of humor. (If you have to put people down or say crude things to make other people laugh, I think you have a weak sense of humor.) Dustin views his locker conversations as ways to build connections with people. He knows when to be serious and when to cut up. Dustin makes funny comments about life—and even makes fun of himself sometimes—but he does his best not to say things that could hurt other people.

[Hand-drawn box labeled: LIST OF CLEAN JOKES]

ONE MORE THING

Not every conversation will be about Jesus, but some will. I believe God will give you the right words to say, but it's important that you've spent some time thinking and praying about your conversations.

"Be ready to speak up and tell anyone who asks why you're living the way you are, and always with the utmost courtesy" (1 Peter 3:15, THE MESSAGE).

How will you respond when someone asks you about your life? Pray about a three-part answer: your life before you met Jesus, what caused you to turn your heart to Jesus, and your life since then.

Trust that God will give you the right words to say, always be ready to speak up, and remember the "locker rule"—you only have three minutes, so make it count.

Now, come see if you can unlock my locker for me.

AAARRR-GGGHHH!

CHAPTER 5 //

MYSTERY MEAT AND MILK-IN-A-BOX

The noise of the crowd is deafening as you walk down the hallway into the belly of the arena. You can feel the walls rumbling with the frenzied emotion that fills the air around you. After making sure all of your gear is on properly and tightened securely, you nod at the person standing next to you. Together, you work open the door to one of the most frightening arenas in modern culture.

The school cafeteria!

Almost everyone I know has at least one horror story of terrible things happening in the cafeteria.

On our first day of high school, my best friend was a little too aggressive while opening his milk carton, and it ripped in half, covering his jeans in the cold liquid. When we got on the bus three hours later, he still had a wet spot, and you could smell sour milk from 15 rows away. Gross.

MY WORST CAFETERIA STORY

How can a Christ-follower live a life that reveals God's kingdom in one of the most feared spaces on a school campus? Cafeteria conversations are different from locker conversations, because you usually have an extended amount of time to talk with people. Within the first few weeks of school, you know everyone's names, their families, their best jokes, and their most embarrassing moments.

But how can you go a little deeper with your conversations? Try thinking about your time in the cafeteria as one yearlong conversation made up of a bunch of 30-minute conversations. Each day has the potential to go a little deeper and get a little more honest. If you need some help getting your mind around this, ask God to help you answer these questions:

- What's going on in my friends' lives, and how does God want me to help?

- How can I help my friends who aren't followers of Jesus be more open to him?

- How can I encourage my Christ-following friends to grow in their faith?

- How do my friends need to see me LaRK (live and reveal God's kingdom) so they will find their place in his kingdom?

KNOWING WHAT'S GOING ON

Many of us like the idea of having deeper conversations with people, but we struggle to know how to help a conversation move beyond social media, music, and homework assignments. How can you be more intentional?

Think about the struggles teenagers face. When and where do you or your friends experience anxiety, fear, loneliness, or uncertainty? Or what things create those challenges in the life of the average teenager in your school?

COMMON STRUGGLES OF TEENAGERS:

Ask Jesus to help you notice the things people don't say. You may have a friend whose experiencing loneliness because his parents are separated. Your friend likely won't say, "I'm feeling alone," but he may say, "I grabbed dinner from McDonald's and ate in front of the TV last night." As you work to get in tune with Jesus, you may be surprised at the things your friends are saying without actually saying them.

LIST 3 FRIENDS WHO ARE HURTING
1. _____
2. _____
3. _____
ASK GOD WHAT YOU CAN DO TO HELP.

Ask Jesus what he wants you to do. Sometimes Jesus helps you see things so you'll pray about them. Sometimes he opens the door to conversations and gives you words to say to help your friend. And sometimes he shows you things in a friend's life and nudges you to do something to help.

GUIDING FRIENDS TOWARD JESUS

Remember, the best thing you can to do to lead someone toward Jesus is live a life that reveals God's kingdom in front of them.

==Your friends will see your life more clearly than they hear your words.==

But as you're LaRKing in front of your friends, there are a few things you can do to help them think more deeply about their own lives.

Ask good questions. One of my heroes once said that for every question we ask and someone answers, we should ask two or three good follow-up questions to understand what that person is really saying and feeling.

TBH *This feels like I'm being manipulative. Can't I just have a normal conversation with my friends?*

Absolutely! In fact, most conversations will continue to look the same. But when Jesus nudges you, and you sense that it's time for your conversations to go a little deeper, you'll be ready.

I love to ask people, "Are you happy with your life?" It opens the door to some deeper conversations in a mostly non-threatening and easy-to-say-yes-to-and-move-on sort of way. Then I follow up with another good question or two.

If your friend says they're happy, ask something like, "Cool! What is it about your life that makes you happy?" And as they begin sharing their thoughts, you'll get to know them—the real them.

If your friend says they aren't happy, ask something like, "What is it about your life that keeps you from being happy?" When someone invites you into spaces like this, listen closely for the Holy Spirit's nudging and try to love your friend the way Jesus loves them.

I also like to ask questions about hot topics. If a pop star does something especially crazy, I'll ask, "What did you think about what so-and-so did at whatever awards show last night?" Or if something political happens in the news, I might ask, "Do you think much about politics? What do you think about what so-and-so said?" Or if a movie or TV show is all the buzz, I'll ask, "Did you see fill-in-the-blank? What do you think about what happened?" Listen carefully to the answers, because they will often give you an idea of what your friends think about other important things.

Be careful. It is super important that you don't get trapped in arguments with friends over topics you disagree on or you'll end up arguing over something that's not essential to the kingdom of God. The resulting frustration could actually push someone away from a relationship with Jesus. I'm not all that concerned if my friends disagree with my views on creation vs. evolution; I want them to make a decision to follow Jesus.

"Your speech should always be gracious, seasoned with salt, so that you may know how you should answer each person" (Colossians 4:6, HCSB).

Give honest answers. Following Jesus is amazing. It's a life filled with wonder, passion, love, purpose, and joy. But at times it's also filled with heartache, disappointment, frustration, loneliness, and pain.

Many people believe if they start following Jesus, their life magically and immediately will become perfect. The truth is, very soon after following Jesus, bad things may happen. And people can assume either God's not real, or God's not good.

==Jesus said his followers should *expect trouble*, because they're his followers.==

"I've told you all this so that trusting me, you will be unshakable and assured, deeply at peace. In this godless world you will continue to experience difficulties. But take heart! I've conquered the world" (John 16:32-33, THE MESSAGE).

LIST OF THINGS IN YOUR LIFE THAT WERE **BAD** BUT GOD TURNED TO **GOOD**.

1. _____
2. _____
3. _____
4. _____

Christ-followers experience all the same junk that everyone else does. The difference? We understand that Jesus promised to be with us to help us get through it—and not simply help us limp through our lives but work everything into something good.

"And we know that God causes everything to work together for the good of those who love God and are called according to his purpose for them" (Romans 8:28).

In the midst of the difficulties of the world, Christ-followers can have peace, because Jesus has overcome the world. Your friends need to know this truth and see you live it out. So be honest about your struggles, your doubts, and your trust in Jesus in the midst of it all.

ENCOURAGING FRIENDS WHO ALREADY FOLLOW JESUS

I remember at times feeling like I was the only person at my school who really loved Jesus. It was a lonely feeling. As I began to share my faith and live a life that revealed God's kingdom, I learned that I wasn't alone. And the odds are, other people at your school are followers of Jesus, too.

What can you do to encourage them?

Show them love. I'm not sure why, but Christ-followers can be pretty mean when another Christ-follower messes up. The truth is, I'm not perfect. And you're not perfect. And your Christ-following friends aren't perfect either. And when I mess up, I don't need someone to tell me how bad I am; I need someone to love me. Just like Jesus loves me.

Pray for them. Right now, I bet people are praying that you'll make good decisions, that you'll be safe, and that you'll live a life that reveals God's kingdom.

We can always benefit from more people praying for us.

Pray for your friends to grow in their trust in Jesus. Pray that Jesus would open doors for them to see his work in their lives. Pray that they are able to forgive others when they've been hurt. Pray that they can forgive themselves when they mess up. And ask them what you can pray for; you might be surprised at their answers.

Pray with them. You might talk to your Christ-following friends and see if they would want to pray together. I love "See You at the Pole," but what would happen if Christ-followers on your campus would start getting together whenever you felt like praying, not just one morning in September?

Pray for your school, the administrators, teachers, and other students. Pray for the safety of sports teams and field trips. Pray for the students who feel alone, that Jesus would open your eyes to see their hurts and give you the courage to respond. Pray like Jesus, that God's kingdom would come to your campus.

Help each other live a life that reveals God's kingdom. When I was in high school, four of my friends and I started an "accountability group." I'm not a huge fan of the word *accountability*, but we all needed help to live the lives we wanted to live, the lives God created us to live—lives that revealed God's kingdom. So we gave each other permission to remind us when we weren't doing the right thing.

"As iron sharpens iron, so a friend sharpens a friend" (Proverbs 27:17).

What could Jesus do in your school if a group of teenagers took their relationship with him seriously enough to start helping one another live lives that reveal God's kingdom?

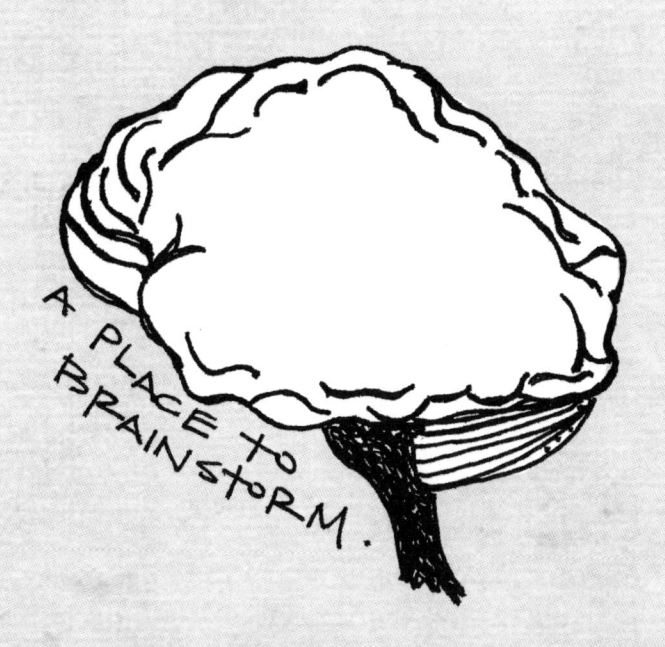

A PLACE TO BRAINSTORM.

HELPING FRIENDS FIND THEIR PLACE IN GOD'S KINGDOM

I find it pretty strange that Jesus uses the language of slavery and servanthood to describe life in the kingdom of God. He said things like...

- The first will be last

- Lose your life

- Give yourself away

Jesus paints a picture of a life that puts others first in order to reveal God's kingdom. It's not a glamorous life by our culture's standards, but God tells us it's the way to find real life.

"It is absolutely clear that God has called you to a free life. Just make sure that you don't use this freedom as an excuse to do whatever you want to do and destroy your freedom. Rather, use your freedom to serve one another in love; that's how freedom grows" (Galatians 5:13, THE MESSAGE).

Paul also tells us that we can work hard to build connections with people based on what they like. He says we can take the initiative to find common ground with others, so we can help them find their place in God's kingdom.

"I try to find common ground with everyone, doing everything I can to save some. I do everything to spread the Good News and share in its blessings" (1 Corinthians 9:22-23).

Living and revealing God's kingdom doesn't mean that we stop being who we are. It means that we become intentional about living lives that show people glimpses of the kingdom of God in ways that meet their specific needs. And when we trust God enough to live this kind of life, we discover more of who we really are.

DUSTIN AND DENNIS

Dennis likes lunch, because he loves to eat and because the cafeteria gives him a chance to become more popular. He uses lunchtime to catch up with friends, to tell lots of jokes, to make fun of other students, and occasionally to catch up on studying. In short, Dennis' lunch is all about Dennis.

Dustin likes lunch, too, because he loves to eat and because he's learned how cool it is to have conversations that matter. Sometimes conversations are about nothing—weekend plans, homework assignments, funny stories. But sometimes God opens a door for a deeper conversation to take place. And when this happens, Dustin knows God is inviting him to partner with the work of God's Spirit in friends' lives. In short, Dustin's lunch is about whatever God wants it to be about.

ONE MORE THING

Conversations like this always feel giant and intimidating and overwhelming. Take a deep breath, relax, and remember that living and revealing God's kingdom is a natural response to God's love in our lives. All of the stuff we talked about in this chapter—and it's a lot—is ultimately about you being in tune with Jesus. As Jesus leads, you follow. As Jesus speaks, you obey.

As Jesus nudges, you respond. And the coolest part of all, living this life is amazing!

You never regret adjusting your life in response to God's leadership. And you can do it.

CHAPTER 6 //

DUSTY BOOKS AND "QUIET PLEASE"

I like the library. I find that it's the best place on campus to sneak a nap.

Just kidding...sorta.

The library means a lot of different things, but to me it symbolizes thinking. It's the place at most schools where you can go to get away from noise and chaos, quiet your mind, and think/read/study/reflect. It's the place where you can put your mental muscles to work and learn.

TBH *So why are we talking about thinking and learning in a book about LaRKing? God doesn't care about our minds, as long as we aren't thinking bad things, right?*

I'm not so sure. Read what Jesus said after someone asked him what was the most important commandment:

*" 'You must love the Lord your God with all your heart, all your soul, and **all your mind**.' This is the first and greatest commandment. A second is equally important:*

'Love your neighbor as yourself.' The entire law and all the demands of the prophets are based on these two commandments" (Matthew 22:37-40; emphasis mine).

Love God with all your mind. And this wasn't something new that Jesus made up; he was quoting from the Old Testament (Deuteronomy 6:5). I especially love how this phrase reads in The Message: *"Love the Lord your God with all your passion and prayer and intelligence."*

What does it mean to love God with your mind, with your intelligence, with your thinking?

Space to Brainstorm

RENOVATE YOUR IMAGINATION

One of the first Bible verses my youth pastor encouraged me to memorize was Romans 12:2...

"Don't copy the behavior and customs of this world, but let God transform you into a new person by changing the way you think. Then you will learn to know God's will for you, which is good and pleasing and perfect."

A while back, my church's pastor shared a message series called "Imagine That." In this series, he suggested that because we are shaped by our experiences, our ability to think creatively about life has been crippled. He challenged each of us to allow God to "renovate your imagination," so that we could begin to see the "what if"s of life instead of assuming the worst. (More on this later in the book.)

For example, think about the bully at your school. Now imagine that she or he showed up to school tomorrow completely changed. Instead of making fun of people, she or he only said kind and encouraging things.

That's probably tough to picture—but why? Why is it so difficult to imagine your school bully changing?

Because we have been shaped by our experiences, and our imaginations have grown dull.

I believe Paul recognized our dullness in Romans 12, and he encourages us to allow God's Spirit to "renovate our imagination"—to give us the gift of seeing *what could be* if we chased the kingdom of God in all parts of our lives.

In the chart to the left, list the three greatest challenges in your life right now. Then consider what each situation could look like if God transformed them into exactly what he would want for your life.

DO THE BEST THINKING YOU CAN

Before you panic, this statement has nothing to do with how smart you are. You are called to do your best thinking because you are called to do your best *everything*. Every part of your life can be an act of worship to God.

"And whatever you do or say, do it as a representative of the Lord Jesus, giving thanks through him to God the Father" (Colossians 3:17).

For me, doing my best thinking means no phone, no computer, no computer, no guitar, no music, no nothing; it's me and my thoughts, and it's usually late at night or early in the morning. Figure out when, where, and how you do your best thinking, and allow God to guide your thoughts, as you love him with your mind.

DUSTIN AND DENNIS

Dennis is pretty smart, so he rarely gets anything lower than a C. If he studied, he could probably get mostly A's, but he only gets grounded if he gets D's or F's, so he feels pretty good about his grades. As long as he shows up to class and does most of his homework, Dennis can coast to a 2.0 GPA.

Dustin is pretty smart, too, and until recently, he was just like Dennis. As long as he didn't get in trouble, he was happy. But lately, Dustin has started sensing that God wants him to do more—not so God will love him more or so God won't zap him, but because Dustin has begun to understand that his intelligence came from God. Dustin wants to work hard to use that gift the best he can.

QUIET YOUR MIND

I can go days at a time without doing *any* thinking, much less my *best* thinking. I know my brain is functioning, and I might even get some basic tasks done, but I'm not really *thinking* about anything. To think well, we have to focus. We have to let our minds be still and quiet. We have to stop filling our time with things that lull us into laziness or distract us.

The main thing that lulls me into laziness is television. I can put on my favorite channel and watch hours and hours of shows.

And my main distraction is the Internet. Social media sites, streaming video sites, online games, researching the kopi luwak coffee bean—all of these things distract my brain from thinking about anything that matters.

Television isn't inherently bad, but it can become a major reason we press "pause" in our brains and become receivers of entertainment. The Internet isn't inherently bad either. In fact, the Internet has the potential to be a great source of learning and a challenge to think more deeply. But we must have the discipline to use TV and the Internet with good intentions and healthy boundaries and not get drawn into using them as an excuse to stop thinking.

Be still. You may have heard something about this before, but it is important to build some time into your schedule to relax. I'm not talking about the time right before you fall asleep, but something deeper.

Psalm 46:10 declares, *"Be still, and know that I am God!"* We sometimes confuse the phrase "be still" with physical movement. And certainly that could be part of what the writer of this psalm means, but the Hebrew word used here—*raphah*—means something more. *Raphah* literally means "to sink" or "to relax." The picture that captures the idea is loosening a rope so instead of being stretched tight, it has some slack in it.

This same verse (Psalm 46:10) in The Message begins, "Step out of the traffic!" That's what we need to build into our schedule. In Chapter 8 we'll talk more about rest, but when it comes to quieting your mind, it's important to take some time to disconnect from the craziness of the world and give your mind space to breathe.

THINK ABOUT GOOD THINGS

I've heard people say that you can't control what you think; I disagree. Yes, random thoughts pop into our mind from time to time, but what are you spending your time thinking about?

Do you sometimes get stuck worrying about all the things that can go wrong in your day? Being aware and responsible is one thing; being consumed with worry is something else—and it's not good.

Are you sometimes preoccupied with what other people think about you? Living a life that reveals God's kingdom is important; allowing people's opinions to shape how you live is something else—and it's not good.

Do you sometimes criticize and judge others in your mind? Observing the choices other people make so you can learn from them is one thing; allowing those observations to cause you to feel superior or more spiritual than other people is something else—and it's not good.

When negative thoughts pop into your head, what do you do with them?

Do you focus and fixate on them, allowing them to dominate your thoughts? Or do you choose to focus on something different—something good?

God defines what is good. In Philippians, Paul tells us what we ought to think about, and he connects our thoughts with the way we live:

"And now, dear brothers and sisters, one final thing. Fix your thoughts on what is true, and honorable, and right, and pure, and lovely, and admirable. Think about things that are excellent and worthy of praise. Keep putting into practice all you learned and received from me—everything you heard from me and saw me doing. Then the God of peace will be with you" (Philippians 4:8-9).

Instead of allowing lies, untruths, and half-truths to shape us, focus on things that are true.

Instead of only thinking about things that are frivolous, think about things that matter.

Instead of dwelling on things that are wrong or bad, fill your mind with God's vision for what things could be.

Instead of allowing your thoughts to be dragged down to inappropriate things, protect your thoughts and keep them pure.

Instead of focusing on negative things that you learned about through hearsay, fix your thoughts on pleasant things that you know are true.

"Think about the things of heaven, not the things of earth" (Colossians 3:2).

Paul isn't suggesting that we turn a blind eye to the pain and struggles in our world; he is encouraging Christ-followers not to focus our thoughts on these and dwell on them. Paul tells us to focus our thoughts on things of the kingdom of God, because only as God's Spirit renovates our imagination can we understand how God wants us to respond to challenging situations.

As people who are striving to LaRK in our daily lives, we can notice the hurts of others and work to bring God's kingdom to all areas of our lives. Our identity as followers of Jesus is to live a life that reveals God's kingdom as a contrast to the world's brokenness.

DON'T THINK ABOUT BAD THINGS

We all struggle with the thoughts that pop into our minds. Sometimes the thoughts are random, and we don't know where they come from. But sometimes the thoughts are from things we've seen in our past—an image, a video, a memory, a conversation, and so on.

==While it may seem that our thoughts are innocent because they "only" affect us, Jesus challenges us to think differently about our thought life.==

Matthew 5 is the beginning of a three-chapter section called the Sermon on the Mount; you could call it the Jesus manifesto. It's Jesus' longest teaching about what is most important in life. In the first half of that chapter, Jesus says that the kingdom of God can be found in every life situation, and our job is to highlight it to the people in our lives—very encouraging and positive stuff. But the second half of Matthew 5 contains some challenging comments:

ANGRY

"But I say, if you are even angry with someone, you are subject to judgment!" (Matthew 5:22).

LUSTFUL

"But I say, anyone who even looks at a woman with lust has already committed adultery with her in his heart" (Matthew 5:28).

The definition for *angry* in verse 22 is a "fixed anger." It's replaying the "scene of the crime" over and over again in your head. It's allowing the anger to simmer in your mind for days or longer. It's holding on to the memory and pain and anger, refusing to let it go.

The definition for *lust* in verse 28 is a "focused-upon desire." It's repeatedly picturing a person doing what you want them to do. If you repeat the idea enough, it becomes difficult to view the person apart from your own desires. It's allowing your thoughts to go to an unhealthy place and stay there.

In both of these examples—and many others throughout the Bible—Jesus is encouraging us to stop thinking bad thoughts. Inappropriate and unhealthy stuff will pop into our minds from time to time, but what do we do with these thoughts? Jesus invites us to think differently—to allow the Holy Spirit to replace all the bad and fill our minds with a kingdom imagination.

TBH

This feels a little fake. How can I NOT think about bad things when there is so much bad stuff going on?

I believe Satan is real; he hates you and wants to destroy you. If he can keep you discouraged by all the bad stuff that's happening, he doesn't have to worry about you living and revealing God's kingdom.

Bad stuff damages our ability to imagine that God can do good stuff.

But what if we allowed God's Spirit to renovate our imagination? What if we recognized that bad stuff was happening, but instead of getting consumed by it, we began praying that God would interrupt the bad with the goodness of his kingdom?

But what about when bad stuff happens to me?

Unfortunately, we can't stop bad stuff from happening. Our world is broken, because God gives people like you and me freedom to make our own choices. Sometimes our choices are good. And sometimes our choices are bad. And sometimes our choices are so bad that they hurt other people. And sometimes other people's choices are so bad that they hurt us.

So what do we do?

We must remember that Satan is real, he hates us, and he wants to destroy us. And Satan will use our bad decisions to hurt as many people as possible. Instead of directing our anger at ourselves or at others for making bad decisions, what if we began praying that God would do something good in the midst of every bad situation?

What if we asked God's Holy Spirit to renovate our imagination and to help us see the good that could be?

ONE MORE THING

$e=mc^2$

EINSTEIN

BALD EINSTEIN

Some people believe that trust in Jesus is only for dumb, weak people—that it's a crutch to help people limp through life. But I hope as you grow in your own life experiences, education, and relationship with Jesus, you will realize a few key truths. God gave you your intellect. God welcomes your questions and your doubts. God wants to stretch your thinking and imagination to new places. And if you learn to love God with your mind *without fear*, I believe you'll experience the wonder and mystery and beauty that can only be found in the fullness of the kingdom of God.

CHAPTER 7 //

TEAM CHEERS, OVERTIME, AND ARPEGGIOS

I decided to follow Christ when I was in the 10th grade. I wasn't a bad guy with a terrible history before that, but I didn't have a clue who Jesus was, or what it meant to trust and follow him. I was living life for myself, and I decided to start living a life that put him in the center. It was a radical transformation.

Up until that point in my life, I was known mostly for my big brother. He was a great football player in high school and at a Division I college. He didn't advance to the next level, but in our hometown, he was (and is still) a big deal.

I liked football, but I wasn't great at it. I started playing when I was in the third grade—partly because I liked it, but mostly because my dad loved it. My high school football memories had more to do with me botching a play (that we later watched and re-watched and re-watched again in our post-game film session; thanks, Coach Farlowe) and begging to be put back in the game than any stellar or memorable plays. Football was my identity, but it wasn't much of one.

When I became a Christ-follower, my whole identity changed.

The way I lived and the reason why I lived that way changed. How I spent my time and the people I spent it with changed. And the reason I played football changed. It was no longer about whether I was a starter or not, or how many plays I aced or botched. I was on the football team because that's where Jesus wanted me, because someone (or several someones) on the team needed to find his place in God's kingdom.

I still made a ton of mistakes—some because I was young and immature, most because I was selfish. I also learned a lot of lessons—some because I did it right, most because I messed up. Looking back, I wish someone had told me some of the things I want to encourage you to do as you strive to LaRK on your team, in your club or band, or in your favorite extracurricular activity.

KEEP JESUS AT THE CENTER OF YOUR LIFE

My oldest daughter tried out for her middle school basketball team. On the first day of tryouts, the coach gave each girl a letter to take home and discuss with her parents. Among the expected comments about team rules, practice and game schedules, and other housekeeping items, we found some pretty alarming comments.

In the letter, the coach basically told the girls that if they wanted to play on his team, they couldn't play any other sports, participate in any other extracurricular activities, or decide to drop basketball until they graduated from high school. He said that a commitment to basketball in the seventh grade was a commitment to play basketball through high school.

What?!?

The basketball coach wanted my daughter to focus on basketball, only basketball, and nothing but basketball. It sounded like he wanted basketball to become her god.

Have you ever heard of that? Sports or clubs or bands or other things being your god?

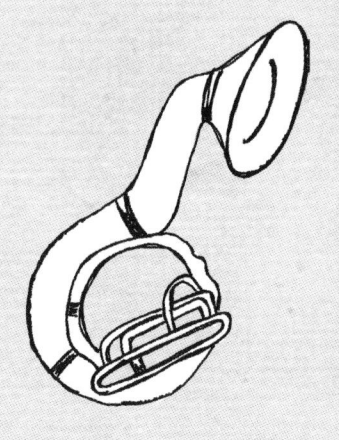

Sports, clubs, bands, and hobbies can teach you lots of life lessons related to teamwork, sportsmanship, and discipline. They also can help you discover talents that you may not have even realized you had. And I believe if you make a commitment to participate in these sorts of activities, you should honor your commitment.

But I also believe you have to navigate all these things while keeping Jesus at the center of your life.

It starts with having a healthy understanding of who Jesus is and what it means to live a life that reveals God's kingdom. And that understanding shapes who you are and what makes you valuable, because we chase things that make us feel significant.

KNOW WHO YOU ARE

Unfortunately, many teenagers believe that their importance comes from places like their accomplishments, their possessions, other people's opinions, or their good behavior. Those things are fine, but if you base your value on these things, what happens when you miss the basket or play a wrong note, when your "friends" turn their backs on you, or when you do something stupid? If you believe those things define your worth, then you start feeling worthless. And when you feel worthless, you begin chasing things that make you feel significant.

But God believes you are priceless. Not because of your accomplishments, your possessions, other people's opinions, or your good behavior.

God says that you are valuable because you are his.

"How precious are your thoughts about me, O God. They cannot be numbered! I can't even count them; they outnumber the grains of sand! And when I wake up, you are still with me!" (Psalm 139:17-18).

You are his creation, made in his image, and he loves you.

"So God created human beings in his own image. In the image of God he created them; male and female he created them" (Genesis 1:27).

God has a plan for your life that is good and pleasing and perfect.

" 'For I know the plans I have for you,' says the Lord. 'They are plans for good and not for disaster, to give you a future and a hope' " (Jeremiah 29:11).

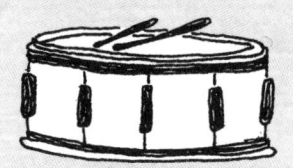

When you understand that your worth comes from God and doesn't change based on anything you do or don't do, say or don't say, have or don't have, you are free to live a life that reveals God's kingdom to the students and leaders on your team, or in your club, band, or extracurricular activities.

BE SALT AND LIGHT

Keeping Jesus at the center of your life is the best way to live. And it's a key step in being salt and light among your leaders and peers. Remember Jesus' words:

"You are the salt of the earth. But what good is salt if it has lost its flavor? Can you make it salty again? It will be thrown out and trampled underfoot as worthless. You are the light of the world—like a city on a hilltop that cannot be hidden. ... In the same way, *let your good deeds shine out for all to see, so that everyone will praise your heavenly Father" (Matthew 5:13-14, 16).*

I love how these two phrases read in The Message:

"You're here to be salt-seasoning that brings out the God-flavors of this earth" (Matthew 5:13).

"You're here to be light, bringing out the God-colors in the world" (Matthew 5:14).

And the reason why we're salt and light:

"Keep open house; be generous with your lives. By opening up to others, you'll prompt people to open up with God, this generous Father in heaven" (Matthew 5:16).

God is at work in the world—God-flavors and God-colors—and he invites us to live lives that help people see him.

Our job is to live and reveal God's kingdom—to LaRK—by keeping Jesus at the center of everything we do.

Be a good teammate. If you're running sprints, run through the line. If you're practicing scales, do them all and get them right. If you're doing homework for a group project, get your stuff done well and on time. Don't cut corners. Encourage others. Give 100 percent no matter what.

Use your talents to honor God. All of your gifts, skills, and talents come from God. Some might argue that it's intelligence and hard work and discipline that develop skills. I would partly agree—developing skills takes effort on your part. But where does the skill originally come from? And who gave you the intelligence to learn? And who gave you the physical capabilities to work hard? And who gave you the discipline to focus and get the work done? All of those things come from God. So use all of those things to honor him.

DUSTIN AND DENNIS

Dennis is a pretty good athlete. He's a natural leader, he's always been in shape, and he's fast. He doesn't see anything wrong with slacking off at the end of his sprints, because he's still faster than almost everyone else on the team. But his laziness also comes out during games, and his coaches wonder where that lack of discipline will show up later in life.

Dustin is a good musician. He's a little quieter than some, but his instrumental skills have earned the respect of his band. And anytime there's something new to be learned, Dustin is the first one to learn it. Sometimes it's easy for Dustin, because he loves music so much. But even when Dustin is busy, he works hard because he doesn't want to let his band down. The band's leader knows the habits Dustin has developed now will help him in every area of life tomorrow.

CONNECTING THE DOTS

When I was a teenager, I felt like I was busy all the time. But when I look at teenagers today, you're 100 times busier than I was, so the idea of adding one more thing to your already-full plate seems overwhelming.

I believe living the kingdom life adds nothing to your schedule except purpose.

I don't believe living and revealing the kingdom of God is a busier life than the one you're living now. If anything, your life may *simplify* as you begin to focus on the things that matter most.

Consider the following Scripture, where Mordecai is talking to Esther, a young Jewish girl who became queen of Persia. In the midst of a devious plot to kill all the Jews under King Xerxes' command, Mordecai challenges Esther with these simple words:

"Who knows? Maybe you were made queen for just such a time as this" (Esther 4:14, THE MESSAGE).

I believe the same statement could be made to each of us:

Who knows? Maybe you are on this baseball team for just such a time as this.

Who knows? Maybe you are in this jazz band for just such a time as this.

24/7 81

Who knows? Maybe you are on this cheer squad for just such a time as this.

Who knows? Maybe you are in this Spanish club for just such a time as this.

And this concept isn't just limited to your hobbies.

Who knows? Maybe you have this part-time job for just such a time as this.

Who knows? Maybe you are at this lunch table for just such a time as this.

Who knows? Maybe you are in this homeroom for just such a time as this.

Who knows? Maybe you live in this neighborhood for just such a time as this.

Who knows? Maybe you are in this youth group for just such a time as this.

Who knows? Maybe you are in this family for just such a time as this.

Who knows? Maybe you are _____ for just such a time as this.

What in your life fills in that blank? Ask God to help you connect the dots of who you are and how he's shaped you to live. What will you do with the opportunity you've been given?

TBH

This whole thing just feels a little dramatic. Couldn't it just be that I like volleyball, so I decided to play volleyball? Does it really have to be something spiritual like you're saying?

I believe all of life is spiritual. You can't separate the spiritual from the non-spiritual. If you're a follower of Jesus, everything in your life is a part of God's story for you. Maybe your first step is to give 100 percent, 100 percent of the time. Maybe your next step is to begin praying for your teammates and leaders. Or ask Jesus to show you some ways you can have a positive impact on your co-workers' lives. Or follow Jesus' leading when he opens a door for you to have an impact. And maybe all these steps take a whole season to unfold. Are you willing to give Jesus a chance and keep him at the center of your life?

ONE MORE THING

Social media has become the central place for teenagers to express themselves and interact with others. In my family, we've established a few questions to help us make sure we're living and revealing God's kingdom through our online identity.

1. Am I being true to God?
2. Am I being true to myself?
3. Am I being true to my family?

These questions serve as a reminder.

I represent God, myself, and my family with every message, photo, or comment I make online.

Spend some time over the next few weeks looking over your past posts. What changes do you want to make in your online behavior to better live and reveal God's kingdom?

Now, go get your cleats on; it's time for practice.

CHAPTER 8 //

STAYING UP LATE AND SLEEPING IN

I'm a night owl. I don't like to go to sleep. I'm always afraid I'm going to miss something exciting as soon as I close my eyes. In real life, on TV, online, *something* is going to happen, and I don't want to miss it. So I stay up late.

Really late.

But when I do finally get to bed, I like to stay in bed. I don't like getting up. Honestly, it doesn't matter if I set my alarm for 6 a.m. or noon—I want to stay there.

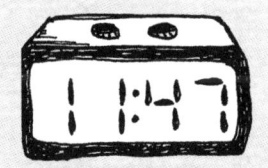

That's why I love Saturdays—the only day of the week when I get to sleep until my body decides it wants to get up.

And I especially loved weekends when I was a teenager. Weekends were days to chill out, to hang out with people I wanted to hang out with, and to do what I wanted to do.

If I could be a teenager again, I'd do my weekends a bit differently. Instead of looking at the weekend as a time to cram everything in that I could, I would slow down a little, do less stuff, and make what I do really count.

TAKE CARE OF YOURSELF

My dad was a hard worker, and he raised my brother and me to be hard workers, too. His job required shift work, so he worked four days, then had four days off, then worked four days, then had four days off, and so on. But "days off" for my dad didn't mean that he didn't work; it meant that he didn't work at his job. He still got up really early, fixed whatever was broken around our house, helped out a friend or neighbor, and found a few chores for me to do.

My dad also played hard. He worked long hours, but he always had time to coach youth football, have a neighborhood cookout, or take the family to do something fun. Work was important to my dad, but play was also important. And play is an important part of rest. I'm so glad my dad taught and modeled this truth to me.

Rest well. In Genesis 1, we read the story of God creating the world. Notice what happens in Genesis 2...

"So the creation of the heavens and the earth and everything in them was completed. On the seventh day God had finished his work of creation, so he rested from all his work. And God blessed the seventh day and declared it holy, because it was the day when he rested from all his work of creation" (Genesis 2:1-3).

Work is important to God, but so is rest.

The Hebrew word for rest is *shabath*—it's where we get the word *Sabbath*. In its purest form, it means "to cease." God stopped; he rested. In Exodus 20:8, God tells us to keep the Sabbath, the "rest day," holy. In that verse, "holy" means "set apart." God wants us to keep a day of rest set apart from other days.

On the Sabbath, God simply wants us to stop doing things we normally do, and spend time doing the things we normally don't get to do. Doesn't that sound pretty restful?

==I believe rest is just as spiritual as work.==

Rest reminds us that we're human, that we live in rhythms, and that we need to set aside some time to stop *doing* and create space in our lives for *being*.

Space to Brainstorm

Make a list of things that you normally don't get to do but you love to do.

Your schedule may not allow you to rest on the weekends. But do you still make time in your schedule to rest? If you don't take care of yourself by resting, your times of school, sports, work, and everything else will be less than they could be.

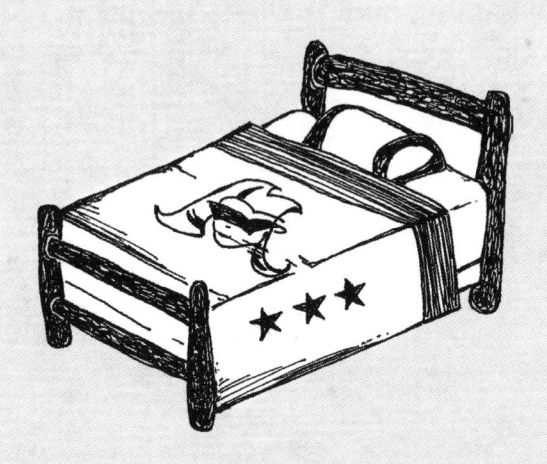

Sleep without distractions. In an age where it seems everyone has computers and cell phones with them at all times, I believe we have lost the ability to get a good night's sleep.

Do you take your cell phone to bed with you? Have you ever replied to a text while almost sleeping and had no memory of it the next day?

Do you compulsively surf online for silly videos, shopping deals, or celebrity news? Have you ever watched an entire television season in one night?

What distracts you from getting a good night's sleep? What can you do to eliminate the distraction? How can you make sure that rest is a priority?

Eat well. If eating were a spiritual gift, my middle name would be Jesus.

Do you love to eat? Is lunch your favorite school subject? Are you the person who finishes off everyone else's food—even if you don't know them?

But do you remember that, ultimately, food is fuel for your body?

Are you eating balanced meals, with proteins, grains, vegetables, fruits, and dairy? Are you eating healthy portions at appropriate times throughout the day? Are you drinking plenty of water?

I'm not suggesting that you should never splurge and occasionally eat something that's less than healthy. But the things we eat matter as we try to LaRK and take care of ourselves.

BE A TEENAGER

I have loved pretty much every age of my life. And while I wouldn't want to go back to being a teenager again, I wish someone had told me to enjoy being a teenager. So let me offer this advice:

Slow down your growing up and enjoy being a teenager!

Space to Brainstorm

List things you can do as a teenager but are difficult to do as an adult.

TBH *Most of the time I think being a teenager is lame. There's so much stuff I can't do until I'm older.*

You're right about having to wait until you're older to do some stuff. But the flip side is, there's a lot of stuff you can only do when you're a teenager. Being an adult is cool, but so is being a teenager. Enjoy the time you have now before the responsibilities and pressure of adulthood take away some of your teenage freedoms.

DON'T BE A STEREOTYPICAL TEENAGER

I hope you know by now that I believe in teenagers. I believe God has a special plan for your life that starts as soon as you embrace it. I believe you're the church of tomorrow AND the church of today. I believe you need the church AND the church needs you.

And I believe you can live life to the full as a teenager and not do all the stupid stuff some teenagers do.

Family stuff. I believe you can have a healthy relationship with your parents. Part of growing up is moving toward adulthood and separating yourself from your parents (see Genesis 2:24), but enjoy your time as a teenager in your family. (Reread Chapter 2 for more thoughts on LaRKing in your family.)

Hanging out with your friends. What's the "cool" thing to do with your friends where you live? I believe it's possible to live and reveal God's kingdom, no matter what you and your friends like to do. (Unless it's illegal or clearly prohibited in the Bible.) But it does require two things from you:

1. Know your standards BEFORE you go places
2. Be strong enough to stand up for what you believe

Example 1. You and your friends go to a movie. Less than 10 minutes into it, stuff starts happening that goes against your standards. (If you need help developing these standards, Ephesians 4:29 and 1 Corinthians 6:18 are good places to start. And I'm sure your youth leaders would love to help you figure this out as well.)

Are you willing to nudge the person next to you and say, "I'm not comfortable watching this—do you want to go wait in the lobby with me?"

What if none of your friends want to leave? What if you're watching the movie at a friend's house? What if they make fun of you for being a prude?

Are you willing to be true to your standards and stand up for yourself in a way that is loving and not shaming?

Example 2. You and your friends go to a party at another friend's house. Pretty soon, music starts blaring, lights go out, and someone pulls out beer and pot.

Are you willing to speak up? Are you willing to grab a friend and leave?

If you don't drive, are you comfortable calling your parents to come pick you up?

What if you're the only one who feels that way? Are you willing to be true to your standards and stand up for yourself in a way that is loving and not shaming?

DUSTIN AND DENNIS

Dennis has been in this situation before, but he wasn't willing to "make waves." A few days later, another friend who was with him said he felt the same way but was too afraid to speak up. Both of them went home regretting their silence and wishing they had done something different. But both know they'll do the same thing the next time it happens.

Dustin has been in this situation, too, and even though he didn't speak up about it, he did call his parents to come pick him up. He wishes he had spoken up, but he's glad he left when he did. He's committed to be a little more outspoken next time.

ONE MORE THING

Just because "everyone is doing it" doesn't mean you have to do it, too. Just because other people have bland, stale imaginations and can't think of better things to do doesn't mean you have to mimic them. Allow God's Spirit to renovate your imagination so you can enjoy your weekends without doing things you'll regret later.

Below is my pretty epic list of 25 fun things to do that are memory makers. Grab a friend or four and get started. (Make sure you get parental permission before you do some of these.)

- Pile into someone's car and take a road trip.
- Try coffee for the first time—or try a new blend of coffee.
- Walk your neighbor's dog.
- Find a playground and relive your childhood.
- Start geocaching (do an online search if you're not sure what that is).
- Make paper airplanes.
- Play tennis at a public park.
- Visit a nursing home.
- Eat food you've never tried before.
- Visit garage sales.
- Go fishing.
- Visit a nearby museum or historical site.
- Go for a bike ride.
- Host a game night.
- Make a music video and post it on social media.
- Have a bonfire. (Definitely make sure your parents are on board with this one!)
- Go to the library.
- Volunteer as a group.
- Have a water fight.
- Plan a flash mob.
- Sleep outside and enjoy nature.
- Do a jigsaw puzzle.

- Watch a whole season of a show from your childhood.
- Go to a local festival.
- Play in the rain.

If my list doesn't seem fun enough, you and your friends can help me out. Send me your ideas at 247book@gmail.com—I'll blog about them and share your brilliance.

Space to Brainstorm

CHAPTER 9 //

SERMON NOTES AND SUNDAY SCHOOL

When I was growing up, church wasn't an important part of my family story. We might show up on Easter or Christmas, but that was about it. And even then, I was so confused by all the standing, sitting, reading, and praying that I checked out in the first two minutes.

So you can imagine my lack of excitement the first time my neighbor invited me to youth group. I was respectful of others' beliefs but had no interest in my own.

My older brother was the same way. Until he started dating a girl who was a Christ-follower. Church suddenly became a high priority in his life. And if my brother was interested in church, I was interested in church, too. What I found when I gave church a chance was amazing.

I found a pastor who seemed to love people. I found a youth pastor who seemed to understand my struggles. I found a youth group with people who—while far from perfect—seemed to try to live differently. I found a Sunday School teacher who seemed to care about me whether or not I showed up for Sunday School, and who kept showing up at my football games. I found a music minister who let me sing a solo, even though I had never sung anything before. I found a handful of other adults who always seemed to be there whenever I needed to talk.

In short, I found a family. I found a relationship with Jesus, a new identity, and a sense of purpose in my life. And it was all wrapped up in this thing called "church."

WHAT CHURCH IS ALL ABOUT

For most of us, "church" means a place—a building where we have a worship service, a Bible study, and maybe an all-night youth event involving marshmallows, frozen turkeys, and sugary, carbonated drinks.

==In the Bible, "church" never means a place. It always means a people.==

"Church" is the group of people who have turned their hearts to Jesus in a relationship of trust. The church is the people—the body of Christ. And it's beautiful.

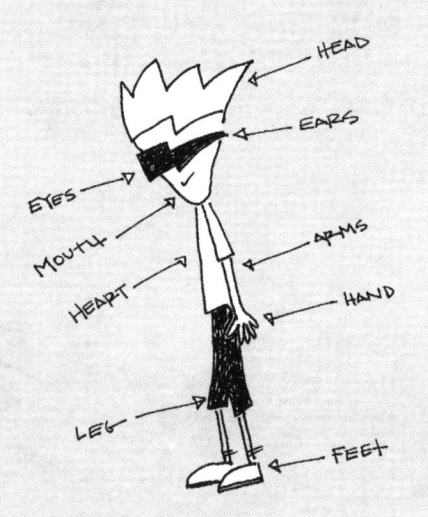

"Just as our bodies have many parts and each part has a special function, so it is with Christ's body. We are many parts of one body, and we all belong to each other" (Romans 12:4-5).

But why have the church? Because God has a mission on earth. God has always had a mission on earth—to fix what was broken in the Garden of Eden. (Read Genesis 3 for a little background.) Jesus came to the world to continue the mission started in the Old Testament.

"This is how much God loved the world: He gave his Son, his one and only Son. And this is why: so that no one need be destroyed; by believing in him, anyone can have a whole and lasting life. God didn't go to all the trouble of sending his Son merely to point an accusing finger, telling the world how bad it was. He came to help, to put the world right again" (John 3:16-17, THE MESSAGE).

The church is the continuation of God's mission to repair all that is broken—God's strategy and plan to redeem humanity and restore all of creation to God's original intent. I don't remember who exactly said this first, but someone really smart once said...

"It is not the church of God that has a mission in the world, but the God of mission that has a church in the world."

Our purpose as Christ-followers is to live lives that reveal God's kingdom to a broken world looking for love and purpose and peace. Twenty-four hours a day, seven days a week.

THE PURPOSE OF A YOUTH GROUP

If the purpose of the church is to live and reveal the kingdom of God and help one another LaRK, then the purpose of a youth group is to help teenagers LaRK in their lives.

So what are some options for your specific role in your youth group?

GEAUX TEAM!

Be a leader. Every group needs someone to step up and speak out first—the teenager who speaks as a peer to other students and says, "We can do this!" in a way no adult leader can.

Are you the leader your group needs?

Be a first follower. Not everyone is wired to be the leader, and that's OK. I believe every group needs a group of "first followers" to say yes when a leader speaks up.

Let me explain.

Renee, a leader, jumps up and says, "Hey everybody, Pastor Brian said he wants us to meet on Main Street and give out free water to people who are stopped at the red light. Let's do it! Who's with me?"

The first follower is the next person who speaks, and I believe that person has more influence on the group than the leader.

In the example above, if the first person to speak after Renee says, "Nobody is going to take water from us. We're a bunch of teenagers," I can almost guarantee you that the idea will die in the next minute. But if the first person says, "I'm in, too! Let's do it," I can almost guarantee you that the idea will be a success, because the first follower sets the direction of the group by their response to the leader.

Are you the first follower your youth group needs?

SUPPORT THE PEOPLE IN CHARGE

Another way you can LaRK in your church and youth group is to be the person who says positive things about the church leaders. Pastors, youth leaders, and other adults whom God has called to lead need encouragement, and that's a gift you can give them.

You can set a positive example by always speaking positively about church leadership. If you have questions or concerns, go talk to the leader about them; don't talk about them with other people.

You can also be helpful by shutting down any negativity you hear. If you hear a student or adult speaking poorly about church leaders, quietly and discreetly encourage them to go and talk to the person they're struggling with instead of sharing their concerns with others.

<mark>Work hard to be a source of encouragement to the leaders in your church and youth group.</mark>

You will be LaRKing when you do it.

TBH *Some of the people in charge in my church are jerks. Or doofuses. Or both. How do I support someone when I don't really like him or her?*

This is a tough question to answer without knowing the whole story. I believe the first best thing you can do is pray about the situation. Then have a face-to-face conversation with the leader(s). I've found that most conflict in my life is addressed by getting to know the heart of the person I'm in conflict with. Beyond that, I'd encourage you to talk with one or two adults who are passionately pursuing Jesus and whom you trust.

CONNECT WITH THE WHOLE BODY

One of the greatest struggles you'll face when you graduate from high school is staying connected with the church. Few churches effectively help their high school graduates prepare to transition to "big church."

Instead of complaining about it, do everything you can to help make that transition as smooth as possible.

Don't just do "youth stuff." Does your church do any festivals or parties or dinners? Grab a few of your friends and join in on the fun. Are there men's nights or ladies' nights at your church? Organize a group of students to be a part of the evening. Just because your youth leaders didn't organize it doesn't mean it won't be a good time.

Appreciate all ages. Research shows that one of the biggest challenges facing the older generations of adults is loneliness. What if you offered to help plan a dinner for older members of your church and recruited other students to help pull it off? What if you and some friends decided to get a list of older members of your church—especially those who can't get out on their own—and started visiting them? Or what if you took this idea one step further and started visiting area nursing homes one Sunday afternoon each month? What an amazing gift you could give of a smile and a little time.

On the other end of the age spectrum, your church probably needs some occasional fill-ins for the nursery or for younger children's Sunday school. What if you and your friends volunteered to be substitute teachers when there's a shortage—or joined the nursery rotation and helped out one weekend each month? You might miss an occasional weekend of youth group stuff, but you'll be blessing to others, and I believe God will bless you as well.

Volunteer to serve. One of the easiest ways to connect with the whole church is through service projects. Is there a workday coming up? Does your church send groups to volunteer with local service organizations? Is there a non-youth-group mission trip coming up that you might enjoy? Don't limit yourself to youth-group-only opportunities to serve others.

And if you're really brave, ask one of your youth leaders—or another adult from your church—to help you find places to serve in your community.

You could be the person God uses to help your entire church get more active in the community through service.

DUSTIN AND DENNIS

Dennis avoids old people no matter what. He likes his own grandparents, but that's about it. And he thinks they smell funny. The idea of choosing to spend time with older adults is nowhere on Dennis' radar. Plus, he doesn't really see the point; even if he doesn't stay connected to church in college, when he gets older he'll come back around. But if you could fast-forward to Dennis at 25, you'd see a different reality: That Dennis has made a ton of mistakes and has hurt a lot of people. He knows he needs to reconnect with God and with his church, but he's so ashamed of the last seven years of his life, he can't bring himself to drive into the parking lot.

Dustin has talked himself out of spending time with older adults all of his life, but something inside of him told him it was time to change that. His church is doing a senior citizen pancake breakfast, and he volunteered to serve. When Dustin's buddy Reynaldo heard he was volunteering, he signed up, too. Fast-forward to Dustin as a 25-year-old, and you'll find Dustin having breakfast in a small diner with five elderly men that he met nine years ago at a pancake breakfast. If you ask Dustin, he would tell you his monthly breakfast with these men is a highlight of his life.

ONE MORE THING —FOR OLDER TEENAGERS ONLY

As you get older, your role in your youth group changes. It becomes less about being served and more about serving others. For example, if you're thinking, "I've heard the same talks for six or seven years—when are we going to talk about something else?" you're still not getting it. Instead of asking, "What is my youth group doing for me?" perhaps you could ask, "How can I live and reveal the kingdom of God in my youth group?" I believe one of the biggest challenges facing youth groups today is the lack of mature upperclassmen living and leading by example. Choose to be part of the solution.

Now elbow your friend and tell them to wake up... church is almost over.

CHAPTER 10 //

FLIRTING, COURTING, AND GOING STEADY

A friend tells the story of Valentine's Day in 10th grade. Early in the day, all the couples at school were holding hands and being smoochy and romantic. By lunch, it seemed like half of the girls were carrying around flowers or stuffed animals that people had given them or—even worse—had sent to the school. By the end of the day, my friend felt like she was wearing a neon sign that said, "I must be messed up, because no one wants to be my valentine."

Ever felt that way? Or felt like no one really liked you, as a boyfriend/girlfriend?

I think most of us have felt this way at some point. But where do these feelings come from? Does God want us to feel unlikable? We know that's not true. So does God want every teenager to be in a dating relationship? You probably know that's not true either.

So what's going on?

I believe our society has created a dating culture that pushes teenagers to move too quickly into relationships, which leads to numerous boyfriends/girlfriends and breakups, which then creates feelings of emptiness and brokenness and forces teenagers into a cycle of one mistake after another and one bad relationship after another.

In short, dating is overrated.

JUST TRYING TO BE HONEST

Let me state two things before diving into our discussion about dating.

First, the things I'm sharing are mostly my opinion. I believe what I'm saying is right, but it's OK if we disagree. I also believe my thoughts have been shaped primarily by the Bible, so if you disagree, ask yourself who or what is shaping your opinion. To be fair, other things shape my opinion, too: stuff I've read and seen. I'm only asking that you consider what I'm saying as an alternative way to think about dating.

Second, most of this chapter will be things you don't want to hear. But just because you don't want to hear something doesn't mean it's not true or good to hear. Keep an open mind and ask Jesus to be clear about any adjustments he might want you to make in your dating life. Maybe he wants to renovate your imagination when it comes to your thoughts about dating.

In this chapter, I want you to do some honest thinking about dating, so you'll notice several places where I've left room for you to brainstorm. Please don't skip over those spaces.

It's important that you develop your own ideas about dating—even if they're different from mine.

RANDOM THOUGHTS ABOUT DATING

I've read a lot of books about dating. But I read all of them after I got married. I wish someone had helped me think differently about dating when I was a teenager. Here are some things I believe now.

As a Christ-follower, you don't have to view dating like everyone else. In our culture, "normal" guys and girls are expected to have girlfriends and boyfriends. Culture says if you're not dating, you're broken. You may not hear those words with your ears, but you've felt them—from music, TV shows, movies, adults in your life, and maybe even your own family and youth group.

I'm not sure I was aware of this pressure as a teenager, but I learned it quickly as a parent. When my youngest daughter was 4, we were hanging out with some friends who had a 3-year-old son. Our kids were playing together, and the mom of the little boy said, "Hey Jonathan (their son), give Ashton (my daughter) a little kiss. She can be your girlfriend!"

So I walked over and punched Jonathan in the face.

Not really. I punched his mom in the face.

Not really. But I wanted to.

I know my friend was trying to be cute, and she didn't really mean anything by her statement. But it illustrates how our culture views dating, even from a very early age. You don't have to view dating like everyone else.

1. WHAT ARE GOOD REASONS FOR DATING?
2. WHAT ARE SOME BAD REASONS FOR DATING?

Space to Brainstorm

Dating isn't inherently wrong; it's just inherently dangerous. What are the *best* things that can happen in a dating relationship? What are the *worst* things that can happen?

Dating has a high level of risk, with a low level of reward, especially if you're in middle school/junior high or early high school.

Remember, dating is overrated. Read my words carefully: I didn't say dating is bad or evil or wrong, just that it's overrated. Don't make it more important than you should.

Space to Brainstorm

1. How does GOD figure into your dating practices?
2. How can these verses help you figure out your thoughts on dating?

Matthew 22:38-40
1 Corinthians 13:4-8a
2 Corinthians 6:14-18
Proverbs 15:22, James 1:5
Jeremiah 29:11

Parents can be very helpful in working out your thoughts on dating. Or not. Some teenagers have great parents who are also great examples of Christ-followers. But other teenagers' parents don't share their values when it comes to matters of faith. You can exceed your parents' expectations when it comes to dating. And you can learn from the things they've done and haven't done—and said and not said.

Dating in groups is almost always best. I believe nearly everything good that can come out of a dating relationship can be found through group dating, with far less risk of crossing a boundary or making a mistake you'll regret.

Being with the right people is important—both whom you date and with whom you group date. What kind of person do you want to date? What is he or she like? What does that person enjoy and value? It's important that you think through these kinds of questions. And it's also important to talk about your thoughts with people you trust and who share your values.

1. Describe the qualities of the person you want to date.
2. With whom can you have open, honest conversations about dating?

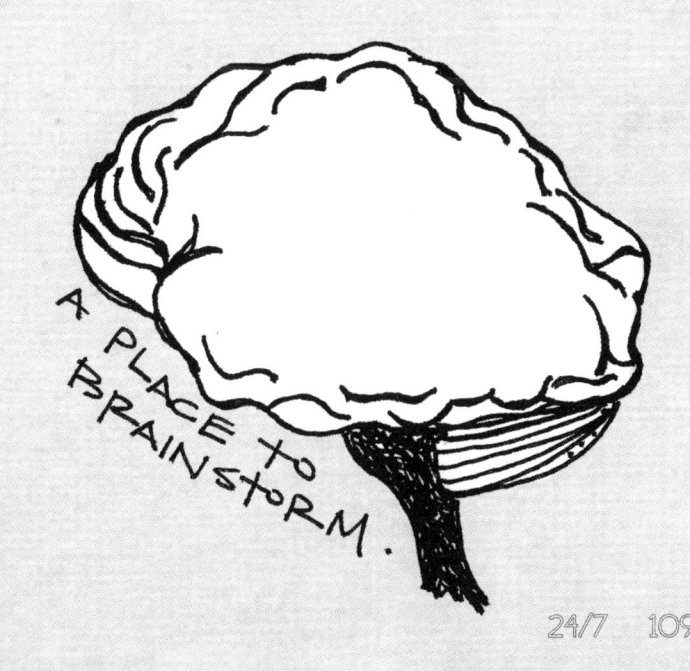

A PLACE TO BRAINSTORM.

It's crucial to set boundaries. Just to avoid confusion, I'm talking about sexual boundaries. God created sex, and it's an amazing gift. But God wants us to enjoy this gift in the way he knows is best: in a committed, loving, marriage relationship. When God warns us about adultery in the Bible, he's not just talking about married people having affairs. I believe adultery is experiencing the sexual side of a relationship with someone who is not your spouse. This includes engaging in sexual activity before you're married.

Dating is and should be about far more than the physical. But because of the nature of adolescence, the physical side of dating is a trouble spot for most teenagers. Setting healthy boundaries is important, because as Christ-followers, we trust that God's way is best.

The best *timing* is to have open, honest conversations with potential dates before you go out. And the best *plan* is set your boundaries before you get into tempting situations. Good intentions tend to fly out of the window once you get into the backseat of the car, or the living room when parents are out of town, or the upstairs room at the party. Decide where you draw the line before you're in a place where it's difficult to think clearly.

1. Do you trust God's plan for sexuality in relationships?
2. What boundaries are you willing to set to help you avoid doing things you'll regret?

Space to Brainstorm

God wants you to live life to the full, and healthy relationships with people of the opposite sex are part of that, even in dating relationships. I still believe dating is overrated. But I also recognize that dating can be a healthy part of your maturity into adulthood. So if you're going to date, date well. Allow God to renovate your imagination about dating, so you don't end up in the same cycle that so many students struggle through while they're in junior high and high school.

LOVE IS A POWERFUL WORD

The first time I said "I love you" to someone was because she said it to me first. I'm not sure if I meant it or not, but I wouldn't have said anything if she hadn't said it first. In other relationships, saying

"I love you" became something I did because I thought it was expected. Plus, it really helped me get out of trouble if I had done something stupid.

Later on, when I really *did* have strong feelings of love for someone, telling her "I love you" felt a little less special, because I had said it so many times to so many others.

I believe it's important to guard our hearts in our dating relationships. I'm not saying that when the time is right that we shy away from sharing our feelings. I'm just saying that in our culture, we say things that we don't fully understand because we feel pressure to say them. Allow God to renovate your imagination, even when it comes to telling someone that you love him or her.

SOMETHING HAPPENS IN YOUTH GROUP

I've seen it countless times. A guy and a girl get really excited about Jesus, and they notice the other person is excited about Jesus, and before you know it, all these feelings about Jesus and each other get jumbled up. Everyone seems to think they're such a perfect "Christian couple," but eventually one or both get distracted from Jesus and start focusing more on the boyfriend or girlfriend. What seemed like the perfect couple starts to drift apart, and two or three weeks go by before you realize neither one are all that excited about Jesus anymore.

And let's not get into how funky youth group feels if they both happen to show up. Awkward.

What am I saying here?

==Be super careful about mixing your passion for Jesus with feelings for a guy or a girl.==

Maybe take this one step further by committing NOT to even consider romance during youth group trips—camps, mission trips, retreats, and so on.

One day God will work out the details of your relationships. Today, keep your focus on your relationship with God, and let the other stuff work itself out down the road.

A GOOD PLAN FOR DATING

As Christ-followers, we need to completely rethink the way we view dating. I've put together a little chart that shows different levels of commitment and what I think is appropriate in each area. Remember, this is my opinion, so it's OK to disagree. I only ask that you allow God to weigh in on your dating decisions.

Stage 1: Hanging Out. The purpose of this stage is to help you figure out what kind of person you are. It's as much about your own process of growing up as anything else. As you spend time with other students of both genders, you grow socially, emotionally, and even spiritually. Hanging out is always done in groups. I recommend waiting until middle school before you start hanging out; your youth group is a great place for hanging out to happen.

Stage 2: Group Dating. The purpose of this stage is to help you figure out what kind of person you most like. It's the time for you to start understanding things like "I like guys who are funny," or "I like girls who are competitive." It's not about finding the right person; it's about finding the right *kind* of person. Group dating is always done in small groups, even if you like one specific person. I recommend waiting until high school before you start group dating, and I'd encourage your whole group to ride together to avoid any one-on-one situations.

Stage 3: One-on-One Dating. The purpose of this stage is to help you figure out if a specific *person* is right for you, if you're right for them, and if Jesus is at the center of your relationship. A lot of significant conversations about things that are important to you now and in the future happen in this dating stage. I recommend waiting until you're a junior or senior or even in college before you start one-on-one dating. And I'd encourage you to get input from several adults whom you trust before moving into this stage with anyone. This stage could last several years, depending on when you start and what your life goals are.

Don't rush it; God's timing is worth waiting for.

Stage 4: Engaged. This stage is reserved for the person you're certain God wants you to marry. Spend a lot of time praying about your relationship before moving into this stage, because the purpose of the "engaged" stage is to help you get to know the family of the person you're engaged to. Even though being engaged is a really big deal, you're still not married. At any point in the engaged stage, if you sense Jesus is not at the center of your relationship, you need to back off. I know quite a few couples who got married because they thought "things will get better after the wedding," only to find that things became more difficult once they were married. You don't marry "potential"; you marry the person God says is right. I recommend waiting until you've begun to get settled into adulthood before getting engaged; who you are in high school and college is different from the person you'll become as an adult. I'd also encourage you to avoid a long engagement; wait until you have a solid sense from God that this is "the one." Then get engaged, and plan your wedding.

Stage 5: Married. This stage is the sweetest space in the whole process, because it's time to give yourself 100 percent to your spouse as God leads the two of you to become one. This is the stage most of us want to experience one day, and the dating decisions you make when you're a teenager will shape the health of your marriage when you're an adult. Before getting married, have lots of conversations with lots of people you trust. God's plan is for one man and one woman to commit themselves to him for life. Even when it's difficult. Even when you feel like quitting. Surrounding yourself with healthy couples and individuals before and after you're married is a huge part of being the person and the couple God wants you to be.

dating timeline

STAGE	PURPOSE	RECOMMENDED AGE
Hanging Out	Get to know the kind of person you are	Middle school/junior high
Group Dating	Get to know the kind of person you like	Early high school
One-on-One Dating	Get to know if a specific person is right for you	Late high school and after
Engaged	Get to know the family of the person you want to marry	Once you're getting settled into adulthood
Married	Give yourself 100 percent to your spouse	Pretty soon after your engagement

TBH

If God created marriage, why do so many married couples seem miserable? Why are people so messed up?

Great questions! In my opinion, marriage is one of the most difficult things you can ever do. But it's also one of the most rewarding things in life. Marriage is a sacred space where you and your spouse give yourselves completely to God and one another. It's vulnerable, risky, passionate, and life-changing. It's really difficult. And it is possible.

50 GOOD GROUP DATE IDEAS

The Internet can be an amazing resource to help you discover creative date ideas. Here are 50 really cool ideas to get you started. And don't forget the 25 fun things to do from Chapter 8.

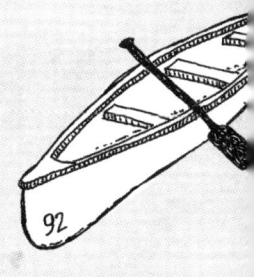

- Go for a walk.
- Go play laser tag.
- Go on a scavenger hunt.
- Go rock climbing.
- Go tree climbing.
- Go mountain climbing.
- Go to a local festival.
- Go to a concert.
- Go see a movie.
- Go to the gym.
- Go cross-country skiing.
- Go waterskiing.
- Go golfing.
- Go mini-golfing.
- Go cycling.
- Go horseback riding.
- Go to a rodeo.
- Go square dancing.
- Go to a zoo.
- Go to an aquarium.
- Go tubing down a stream.
- Go tubing in the snow.
- Go fishing.
- Go ice fishing.
- Go ice-skating.
- Go roller-skating.
- Go sledding.
- Go boating.
- Go rappelling.
- Go backpacking.
- Go on a nature walk.
- Go bird watching.
- Go on a hayride.
- Go hunting.
- Go off-roading.
- Play doubles tennis.
- Play volleyball.
- Play racquetball.
- Play red rover.
- Play hopscotch.
- Play croquet.
- Play basketball.
- Play football.
- Play soccer.
- Play ultimate.
- Play disk golf.
- Play table tennis.
- Play board games.
- Play in the mud.
- Play hide and seek.

TBH *This whole chapter seems lame and old fashioned. We're in the 21st century, and things have changed. What's wrong with casual sex if we both agree to it? And what's wrong with having sex if you're in love?*

I don't have a great response to these questions that I can fit in a paragraph or two. In general, I believe our experiences and our culture have shaped our imagination about dating, so it's foreign to think about dating in the ways I've described in this chapter. But just because our culture says something is normal and OK and right doesn't make it normal and OK and right. God gave us the gift of sex, and there's so much more going on than just the physical side of intercourse. (Just for fun, do an online search for "yada to know.") As we learn God's plan for sex, we must also ask God's Spirit to renovate our imagination so we can think differently about dating.

If you're brave enough, talk to your pastor or youth leader about God's plan for sex. And if you're too nervous about that, email me at 247book@gmail.com.

DUSTIN AND DENNIS

Dennis thinks we're making a big deal out of nothing. He doesn't like being alone, so he's dated lots of girls. Most of them were pretty innocent—one or two dates and that's it, even though Dennis told his buddies some things that weren't exactly true. A few were serious, and they crossed some lines that they later regretted, but they didn't think much about it at the time. They thought they were in love, so they did things they thought people in love were supposed to do. No one told Dennis there was a different way to look at dating.

Dustin is pretty innocent. He didn't have his first date until his sophomore year and his first girlfriend until his junior year. His parents didn't talk to him about dating, but he asked his youth leader and some of his buddies, and his friends all decided that they would hang out a lot as a group and not get wrapped up in dating relationships. That turned out to be a good decision. They also committed to trust God's plan for sex and wait until they were married. A lot of people teased Dustin and his friends about their decision, but they stuck to it. Dustin says he only was able to keep his commitment by avoiding tempting situations and because of his friends' support.

ONE MORE THING

Pornography is a problem. In popular culture, it's normal. But in reality, it's deadly.

Look, this book is almost done, and I have tried to be honest and open about everything. I haven't tried to scare you or bully you or freak you out. I've done my best to share truth in love.

But pornography is dangerous. There's a lot of science behind how looking at pornography changes the way your brain works, and it's scary. There's research that shows the progression of pornography, how it starts with somewhat innocent images/videos, moves into something more explicit, and then becomes a consuming habit.

==If you're struggling with pornography, you need to get some help.==

You need to find an adult you trust and tell them about your struggle. You need to put some safeguards in place that help you make better decisions. You need to respect that pornography is an addiction that takes work to overcome.

No one is perfect in this area. Because God created sex, sexual desire is a natural and powerful human emotion. But unless we experience it the way God designed, we will cheat ourselves and our loved ones out of the gift that God intends sexuality to be.

The best way I've found to help address this issue is through xxxchurch.com. Ask someone for help. Have courage. Take the first step. Begin the process of healing. And enjoy relationships the way God designed.

Now cancel your weekend date and both of you go hang out with a group of your friends.

CHAPTER 11 //

WHAT DO YOU WANT TO BE WHEN YOU GROW UP?

Every child is born with an active imagination. Spend a few minutes watching kids on a playground to see what I mean. With the blink of an eye, children are in a spaceship to the moon, then on a pirate ship in the Caribbean, then climbing a mountain in a snowstorm. They are playing cops and robbers and monkey on the ground and jeep safari before you can set up your lawn chair.

Space to Brainstorm

What was your favorite childhood game?

But if we're not careful, something happens as we get older that dulls our imaginations, shortens our creativity, and weakens our dreams.

It's your job to make sure you never stop dreaming.

NEVER STOP DREAMING

In Romans 12:2, the Apostle Paul wrote that God wanted to transform us by "changing the way [we] think." The Greek word here is *noús*. Scholars define this word like this:

Noús is the God-given capacity of each person to *think*; mental capacity to exercise reflective thinking; the organ of *receiving God's thoughts*, through *faith*.[2]

Another way to understand Romans 12:2 is that God wants to renovate our imagination.

Creativity allows us to see what is yet unseen.

The kingdom of God is the life God dreams for us and invites us to live, and it's amazing and wonderful and passion-filled. But it requires God's Holy Spirit to renovate our imagination so we can see it.

This idea is not new.

After Jesus appeared to two men on the road to Emmaus and blew their minds, he reappeared to them, and...

2: From HELPS™ Word Studies © 1987, 2011 by Helps Ministries, Inc.

"Then he opened their minds [noús] to understand the Scriptures" (Luke 24:45).

Jesus opened up the imaginations of his disciples so they could see what he saw.

Paul elaborated on this idea of renewing our imagination.

"Since you have heard about Jesus and have learned the truth that comes from him, throw off your old sinful nature and your former way of life, which is corrupted by lust and deception. Instead, let the Spirit **renew your thoughts and attitudes** [noús]. Put on your new nature, created to be like God—truly righteous and holy" (Ephesians 3:21-24; emphasis mine).

You will encounter plenty of people in your life who will discourage your dreams: "It can't be done." "Stop being so idealistic." So don't be afraid to ask God's Spirit to renovate your imagination.

==Don't be afraid to think differently and imagine something that is yet unseen. Never stop dreaming.==

DON'T RUSH ADULTHOOD

In Chapter 8, we talked a little about not growing up too fast. Reread that section (page 89), and then come back here.

Go ahead, I'll wait.

Seriously. Go read it.

OK, what was the last sentence in that section? That's right, it was, "Slow down your growing up and enjoy being a teenager!" But how do you do that?

PROTECT YOUR "KID"

I have three daughters. When they were younger, my wife and I struggled to balance protecting them from the bad stuff that could happen, while giving them enough freedom to learn some lessons. We understood that our role as parents was to help our kids grow less dependent on us as they grow more dependent on God (see Chapter 2). But we struggled to teach them how to make good decisions for themselves when we weren't around.

Here's what we came up with.

Everyone is born full of "kid." You only have so much "kid," and when it's gone, it's gone. There are certain things you learn or see or do that take some of your "kid" away. Sometimes it's appropriate to lose some of your "kid"—it's not normal for a 40-year-old to act like a little kid all the time.

==But you don't want to lose your "kid" too soon, because once your "kid" is gone, you can't get it back.==

You can tell when someone doesn't have much "kid" left—they're grumpy, they're impatient, they're inappropriate, and they seem miserable. But when someone has a lot of "kid" left, they're happy, they smile a lot, they like to have fun, and people like to be around them.

This simple idea changed the way we think and talk about decisions, because protecting your "kid" is important.

When our daughters want to watch a movie that is questionable, we ask them, "Do you think watching that movie will take your 'kid' away?" When our daughters tell us about some things one of their friends is doing, we ask, "If you do that, do you think it'll take your 'kid' away?" They think about it, and most of the time—but not always—they make the right decision. Sometimes we overrule their decision and say no, but most of the time we give them the option, and they make a good decision.

For us, this has done two things:

1. Our children have learned to filter their decisions according to whether or not something will take their "kid" away, and if it's appropriate. For example, when it was time to talk to our oldest daughter about sex, she asked us, "If we talk about this, will it take my 'kid' away?" My wife and I thought about it, and

we answered, "Yes, it will take some of your 'kid' away, but you're getting older, and it's OK." She wants to protect her "kid."

2. Our children make decisions that are good for others. For example, my wife and I overheard our younger two daughters talking about watching a TV show. Our middle daughter said, "Let's not watch this show right now, because I wouldn't want it to take *your* 'kid' away." She wants to protect the "kid" in others.

I'm an adult, and I have a lot of "kid" left. But even as an adult, there are things I could see or do that would take some of my "kid" away. So even as an adult, I still protect my "kid."

Make sure you protect your "kid" by making good decisions—now and as you move into adulthood.

LIVE WITH TOMORROW IN MIND

If you're familiar with the teachings of Jesus, that heading may seem like a contradiction to what he spoke:

"Give your entire attention to what God is doing right now, and don't get worked up about what may or may not happen tomorrow. God will help you deal with whatever hard things come up when the time comes" (Matthew 6:34, THE MESSAGE).

I completely agree with Jesus (duh!), but it's important to you understand this:

==The decisions you make today shape who you become tomorrow.==

What are you doing today that will *help you* in the future? How are you honoring the relationships that mean the most to you? What spiritual habits are helping you grow in your trust in God? How are you caring for your physical body today in a way that you'll continue to care for your body tomorrow? How are you keeping your mind sharp and growing and learning? And what new habits can you develop in each of these areas?

```
AREAS to GROW:
PHYSICAL - _____
_____
MENTAL - _____
_____
EMOTIONAL - _____
_____
SPIRITUAL - _____
_____
```

The flip side of this conversation is just as important: What are you doing today that will *hurt you* in the future? What habits have you developed that will damage your relationship with God or relationships with the people that mean the most to you? How are you abusing your body today in ways that could have devastating effects tomorrow? What are you pouring into your mind by the things you listen to, see, read, and watch? What habits do you need to kill in each of these areas?

> **Things to stop:**
> Physical —
> Mental —
> Emotional —
> Spiritual —

The decisions you make today shape the person you become tomorrow. Be wise in your decisions.

MY FAVORITE QUESTION

I don't remember who first asked me this question, but it's something I think about often:

If you could do anything for God, and you knew you wouldn't fail, what would you do?

If you have an answer already, have the courage to get started. If you're not sure, start thinking and praying and talking about it with some friends, asking God's Holy Spirit to renovate your imagination. If you don't have a clue, keep growing in your relationship with God and ask yourself again in a few months.

TBH

I love the idea of God "renovating my imagination," but I'm not sure where to start. Can you help?

Absolutely. I believe God wants to give you the life that, deep down, you've always wanted. I don't believe God hides it from us. In fact, I believe God is constantly inviting us to partner with him as he works in our lives and in other people's lives. That's the whole idea behind living and revealing his kingdom. The one thing God asks of us is trust. So I encourage teenagers (and adults!) to work on deepening their trust in God. And I believe the best way to do that is by practicing spiritual habits. The habits aren't magical, but they put you in a position to trust God a little, then a little more, then a little more, and so on.

Growing in your trust in God takes time, but there are a few THINGS you can do to help:

T – *time with God daily*

H – *honest friendships*

I – *involvement with the church*

N – *notice and serve others*

G – *give to God*

S – *share your God-story (what God has done and is doing in your life)*

Just like a tree that needs the right environment to grow, those six THINGS put you in a place to grow deeper in your trust in God.

DENNIS

Dennis is in his 40s now. He's a divorced dad who sees his kids every other weekend and on Wednesdays for dinner. He doesn't have a lot of real friends, because he doesn't do much. He's a moderately successful accountant at a firm in his hometown, but he doesn't hang out with his work friends. He still attends church occasionally, but he slips out before anyone really notices him. He has dinner with his mom most Sundays, he watches a lot of TV, and he likes to cook. And that's about it.

Dennis has a fair number of regrets from his past, especially in his relationships. He never outgrew his desire to be accepted, so he never developed a true sense of who he is. Depending on where Dennis is, he can blend in pretty well.

Dennis has a gnawing sense of unhappiness. He might not admit it, but deep down, he knows it's true. He's not miserable, but he's stuck, and he has no idea how to get unstuck.

Dennis is leading a normal, forgettable life, and it all started in high school.

DUSTIN

Dustin is in his 40s, too. He's happily married to his college sweetheart (they met at a Bible study). They have two kids who are both followers of Jesus. Their family isn't perfect, but they have a deep love for each other rooted in a deep love for Jesus.

Dustin coaches girls' basketball and teaches PE at a local high school, and he and his wife volunteer in their church's youth ministry. Most weekends you'll find them hosting a cookout in their backyard, usually with a few families joining them. Several nights a week Dustin gets a call from a former athlete or student from church. Sometimes it's because they need advice, but sometimes it's just to check in.

Dustin isn't wealthy, but he's happy. His life is filled with people he cares about, his schedule is filled with things that help others, and he's making a difference in his community.

Very few people outside of Dustin's hometown know him. And he's OK with that. What Dustin doesn't realize is that when he retires, hundreds of former students will come to his party, and they will tell stories of how Dustin changed their lives. Truthfully, Dustin won't remember most of the conversations the students share, but Dustin knows whenever God nudged him to do something or say something, he said yes.

Dustin is living a life that reveals God's kingdom, and it all started in high school.

WHO WILL YOU BE?

You're at a place in your life where you can set the course of who you are and who you will become. Spend some time writing out the future you want for your life.

WHAT I WANT FOR MY FUTURE

WHAT I WANT FOR MY FUTURE

WHAT DO YOU WANT TO BE WHEN YOU GROW UP?

Now spend some time writing down the things you need to do to become the person you want to be.

WHAT I NEED TO DO TO DISCOVER MY FUTURE

FINAL THOUGHTS

I've been praying for you as you've read this book. I've been praying that you will sense in yourself what God believes about you. I've been praying that as you trust God, all of the dreams of your life will be made clear and come true. And I've been praying that God renovates your imagination to see your life through his eyes, a life that reveals his kingdom, 24/7.

"When I think of all this, I fall to my knees and pray to the Father, the Creator of everything in heaven and on earth. I pray that from his glorious, unlimited resources he will empower you with inner strength through his Spirit. Then Christ will make his home in your hearts as you trust in him. Your roots will grow down into God's love and keep you strong. And may you have the power to understand, as all God's people should, how wide, how long, how high, and how deep his love is. May you experience the love of Christ, though it is too great to understand fully. Then you will be made complete with all the fullness of life and power that comes from God.

"Now all glory to God, who is able, through his mighty power at work within us, to accomplish infinitely more than we might ask or think. Glory to him in the church and in Christ Jesus through all generations forever and ever! Amen" (Ephesians 3:14-21).

Let's keep in touch.